D0175838

THE OLD TESTAMENT

SPARK PUBLISHING

© 2002, 2007 by Spark Publishing, A Division of Barnes & Noble

This Spark Publishing edition 2014 by SparkNotes LLC, an Affiliate of Barnes & Noble

All rights reserved. No part of this publication may be reproduced, stored in a retrieval system, or transmitted in any form or by any means (including electronic, mechanical, photocopying, recording, or otherwise) without prior written permission from the publisher.

122 Fifth Avenue
New York, NY 10011
www.sparknotes.com

ISBN 978-1-4114-6965-5

Please submit changes or report errors to www.sparknotes.com/errors.

Printed in Canada

10 9 8

CONTENTS

CONTEXT

THE OLD TESTAMENT IS THE FIRST, longer portion of the Christian Bible. It is the term used by Christians to refer to the Jewish scriptures, or Hebrew Bible. The Old Testament is not one book written by a single author, but a collection of ancient texts written and re-written by numerous authors and editors for hundreds of years. They tell the story of the ancient Israelites, or Hebrew people, and contain the laws and rituals that comprise their religion. For Jews, the collection comprises the *Torah*—the law for worship and everyday living—as well as the history of God's promise to them. For Christians, the Old Testament is also sacred, but they view its religious meaning as incomplete without the life and teachings of Jesus Christ as related in the New Testament. Muslims trace their religious roots to some of the figures in the Old Testament, although they deny the religious significance of the work as a whole. In general, the Old Testament is essential to the way Western civilization has long thought and talked about God, as well as ethics, justice, and the nature of the world.

In its current form, the collection of the Old Testament books was completed by the first century B.C. The individual books themselves, however, are much more ancient—some dating to the tenth and eleventh centuries B.C. or earlier. Because these works purport to tell the history of human origins, many of the events occur much earlier and cannot be historically verified. Later interactions between the nation of Israel and the ancient world, however, can be verified, and historians use these dates to approximate the biblical events. It is estimated that the chronology of the Old Testament covers more than 1500 years, from approximately 2000 B.C. to 400 B.C.

The setting of the Old Testament is the ancient Near East (or Middle East), extending from Mesopotamia in the northeast (modern-day Iraq) down to the Nile River in Egypt in the southwest. The majority of the events take place in Palestine, the ancient land of Canaan—the eastern Mediterranean region stretching seventy-five miles west from the sea and marked by the Jordan River Valley, which runs down the heart of the mountainous land. Situated between the sprawling Egyptian Empire to the south and the Hittite and Babylonian Empires to the north and east, the area was an important trade route in the second millennium B.C. A variety of peoples, mostly nomadic herding communities, scattered the plains. They established small fortified cities, worshipped various deities, and farmed. The inhospitable region prevented any one nation from dominating the area, but the inhabitants were generally called "Canaanite," speaking versions of a common Semitic language, including the languages now known as Hebrew and Arabic.

Very little is known about the early existence of the Israelites outside of the biblical story. In fact, there are no references to Israel in ancient texts prior to 1200 B.C. The Old Testament explains that the Hebrew people (the term used for the Israelites by non-Israelites) were the descendants of a Semitic man named Abraham, who moved to the land of Canaan in obedience to God. Ancient references to a group of outcasts and refugees known as *habiru* exist, but there is little evidence to indicate that these were the Hebrew people. The biblical story tells how the Israelites suffered as slaves in Egypt for many years, and how they miraculously emigrated to Canaan, where they conquered the land and its people in a sweeping military campaign. If true, modern scholars believe this migration may refer to the thirteenth or twelfth century B.C., when a vast upheaval probably occurred in the urban communities of the Canaanite region. However, it is unlikely that a violent or swift conquest by the Israelites took place. Historians believe that the Israelites may have been a part of a gradual, peaceful resettlement, or even a peasant uprising.

The glory of the Israelites in the Old Testament is the vast, united kingdom of David and his son, Solomon, who established a royal capital in Jerusalem, erected a grand temple, and expanded Israel's borders to the Euphrates River. According to the order of biblical events, David and Solomon's kingdoms probably existed around the tenth century B.C. The historical existence of such an Israelite empire is unclear; but after this point, the nation of Israel began to surface in the events of the ancient Near East. The Old Testament describes the tragic division of Israel into two kingdoms and the litany of evil kings who eventually caused the Israelites' demise at the hands of the Assyrian and Babylonian Empires. Historical evidence corroborates some of these events. The northern area of Israel was captured by the Assyrian Empire in 722–720 B.C. The southern area of Israel, called "Judah," was conquered by the Babylonian king Nebuchadnezzar, who destroyed the legendary city of Jerusalem and its temple from 589–586 B.C. A large population of Israel's

CONTEXT

upper class—including artisans, rulers, and religious leaders—were exiled and resettled in Babylonian territory.

The period of the Israelites' exile proved extremely important to the formation of Judaism as an organized religion. The Jewish community's need to retain its identity in a foreign land prompted great theological and literary developments. Much of the Old Testament, especially the religious laws and prophecy, was written whole-cloth or rewritten and edited at this time. The experience of the exile caused the Old Testament writers to define the Torah, or God's laws, and to emphasize biblical themes like suffering and the reversal of fortune. When Babylon fell to the Persian Empire in 539 B.C., the Persian king Cyrus permitted the Jews to return to their homeland. The biblical books of Ezra and Nehemiah (neither of which is discussed in this study guide) document the return of the Jews to Jerusalem under Ezra's leadership, sometime around 460–400 B.C. The impoverished Jews rebuilt Jerusalem and erected a second temple, identifying themselves as a religious community and following the laws of the Torah.

Israel's history and geography is thus crucial to an appropriate understanding of the Old Testament. The region in which the biblical events take place was an area of constant ethnic and political change. The Old Testament depicts the Israelites as a separate and enduring entity throughout this change—a race of Hebrew people descended from one man, possessing a divine right to the land, and distinguishable from the surrounding peoples by its monotheism, or worship of one god. Whether or not these claims are true, the Israelites certainly existed as a people, and the Old Testament remains one of the most vivid pictures of the historical, religious, and literary life of the ancient Near East.

As a work of literature, the Old Testament contains many literary forms, including narrative and poetry, as well as legal material and genealogies. Critics often use terms such as *epic, myth,* and *legend* to classify the biblical stories, as well as describing the heroes, dialogue, and symbols within the text as examples of its literary qualities. Such concepts represent modern and classical ways of understanding literature and were most likely foreign to the authors of the Old Testament. Nevertheless, the Old Testament itself greatly influenced the way Western civilization has thought about literature and stories. As a result, describing the biblical stories through literary terminology remains an important way of understanding the significance of the Old Testament as literature.

STRUCTURE AND COMPOSITION

The Old Testament contains thirty-six books, three of which are separated into two volumes, rendering a total of thirty-nine individual books. The Hebrew Bible divides the books into three main categories: the Pentateuch, the Prophets, and the Writings. In addition to the Old Testament books accepted as scripture by Jews and Protestants, Catholics consider seven "deuterocanonical" books to be scripture. Because the authors of the Old Testament books are largely unknown, scholars believe that the final form of the books indicates the work of "redactors," or editors, who performed a practice common in ancient near eastern literature. The redactors combined previously existing writings, oral traditions, and folktales, and added their own material, to compose the completed books. Often, the redactors attributed a book or a group of books to a significant biblical figure to add validity to their work.

The Pentateuch (Greek for "five scrolls") comprises the first five books of the Old Testament—Genesis, Exodus, Leviticus, Numbers, and Deuteronomy. The collection of books was probably in its final form by the fourth century B.C. The Pentateuch represents the most important section of biblical narrative. It explains the origins of the human race and the rise of the Israelites, including the Israelites' miraculous emigration from Egypt. More than half of the Pentateuch is devoted to God's laws and commandments to Israel. Jews call these books the *Torah,* or law, because of its religious precepts and for the model of ethical behavior that the leading characters prescribe.

Moses, the hero of the Pentateuch, was traditionally assumed to be the work's author. However, modern scholars describe the Pentateuch as the time-worn product of four ancient writers and editors, each of whom revised and expanded existing work. Scholars label the unknown contributors "J," "E," "P," and "D," and identify "J" as the oldest writer, a scribe in King David's court. Different parts of the narrative and laws in the Pentateuch are ascribed to each contributor based on differences in the style and theology of the text.

The second category of Old Testament books comprises the Prophets. Many of these works were composed during or after Israel's exile in the sixth and fifth centuries B.C. The books can be divided into two further categories: the Former Prophets and the Latter Prophets. The Former Prophets are sometimes called the "Historical Books" because they continue the story of the Israelites from the death of Moses to the fall of Jerusalem in 587 B.C. The four works—Joshua, Judges, 1 and 2 Samuel, and 1 and 2 Kings—follow the Pentateuch in the Christian Bible. Scholars sometimes surmise that, together, these books represent the work of a single, unknown editor labeled the "Deuteronomist," who combined separate stories and added work of his own to form a coherent history of the Israelites. The Latter Prophets (which are not covered in this study guide) include the fifteen books of Isaiah, Jeremiah, Ezekiel, and twelve "Minor Prophets." Written before or during the Israelites' exile, these difficult works include sayings and oracles about Israel's downfall, its salvation from exile, and theology.

The Writings denotes the final category of the Hebrew Bible, collected in its present form around the first century B.C. Some of these books are later works chiefly concerned with Israel's history during and after the exile, such as Lamentations, Esther, Daniel, Ezra, and Nehemiah (most of which are not covered in this study guide). With the exception of Ruth and the two books of Chronicles, the remaining books—Job, Psalms, Proverbs, Ecclesiastes, and Song of Solomon—represent the biblical books of poetry and wisdom and are placed after the Historical Books in the Christian Bible. Some are quite ancient, and many represent collections of traditional poems and sayings attributed by a later editor to King David or King Solomon.

Roman Catholic and Greek Orthodox versions of the Old Testament contain an additional category of books called the "deuterocanonical writings," or "Apocrypha." These fifteen books were included in the Septuagint, the Greek version of the Jewish scriptures translated by scribes in Alexandria, Egypt, between the third and first centuries B.C. The Apocrypha contains additional works of poetry and wisdom and, more importantly, stories about Israel during the Greek and Roman periods. These works were not included in the Hebrew Bible, but they were included in the canon, or list, of Old Testament books accepted by the early Christian church. They were later excluded from Protestant versions of the Old Testament following the Reformation in the sixteenth century A.D., and are not included in this study guide.

OVERVIEW

THE OLD TESTAMENT IS A COLLECTION of thirty-nine books about the history and religion of the people of Israel. The authors of these books are unknown, and each book possesses a unique tone, style, and message. Individually, they include stories, laws, and sayings that are intended to function as models of religious and ethical conduct. Together—through hundreds of characters and detailed events—they represent a unified narrative about God and his attempt to relate to humankind by relating to a specific group of people.

The Old Testament contains four main sections: the Pentateuch, the Former Prophets (or Historical Books), the Writings, and the Latter Prophets. This study guide covers books from the first three sections.

THE PENTATEUCH

The Pentateuch comprises the first five books of the Old Testament. It depicts a series of beginnings—the beginning of the world, of humankind, and of God's promise to the Israelites.

Genesis, the first book, opens with God's creation of the world. The perfect world falls into evil when humans disobey God, and the human population divides into separate nations and languages. After many generations, God speaks to a man named Abraham. God makes a promise, or covenant, with Abraham to make his descendants into a great nation and to give them a great land. Abraham shows strong faith in God, and God seals his promise with a number of signs and tests. This special covenant with God passes on to Abraham's son, Isaac, and to his grandson, Jacob. Together, they represent the patriarchs, or fathers, of the Israelite people. Jacob's twelve sons move to Egypt after the youngest brother, Joseph, miraculously becomes a high official in Egypt.

In the Book of Exodus, the descendants of Jacob's children have become a vast people, but the Pharaoh of Egypt holds them in slavery. God chooses one man, Moses, to rescue the Israelites. God sends ten plagues to Egypt, and, with miraculous signs and wonders, Moses leads the people out of Egypt and across the Red Sea. They go to Mount Sinai, where God appears in a cloud of thunder over the mountain and affirms to the Israelites the promise he made to Abraham. God commands them to worship only himself, and he gives them various ethical and religious laws.

The books of Leviticus, Numbers, and Deuteronomy continue the explanation of God's religious laws and his promises to the people. The people must keep these laws to enter and enjoy the promised land, toward which they are heading. Despite God's presence, the Israelites complain and disobey incessantly, inciting God's wrath. They wander the wilderness for forty years in search of the promised land. These books continue the period of Moses's legendary leadership and miracles, until his death at the end of Deuteronomy.

THE FORMER PROPHETS

The Former Prophets, or the Historical Books, cover the history of the Israelites from Moses's death to the fall of the nation in 587 B.C. In the books of Joshua and Judges, the Israelites successfully conquer the land promised to them by God, but they disobey God by worshipping the deities of the surrounding peoples. Neighboring nations invade and oppress the Israelites. God saves the people of Israel by designating judges, or rulers, to lead the people in warding off their enemies.

The two books of Samuel (First Samuel and Second Samuel) cover the rise of the united kingdom of Israel. Israel's religious leader, Samuel, appoints a king named Saul. Saul disobeys God, however, and God chooses another man, David, to be Israel's king. King Saul attempts to kill the young David, but fails. Saul's death closes the first book. In the second book, David establishes the great kingdom of Israel. He conquers Israel's surrounding enemies and establishes Jerusalem as the religious and political center of Israel.

The books of Kings (called 1 Kings and 2 Kings) trace the decline of Israel's success. God blesses David's son, Solomon, with immense wisdom. As king, Solomon expands Israel into an empire and builds a great temple in Jerusalem. Solomon disobeys God by worshipping other deities, and, at his death, the kingdom splits into a northern kingdom, Israel, and a southern kingdom, Judah. A host of evil kings leads the two kingdoms away from worshipping God. Despite the attempts of the prophets Elijah and Elisha to halt Israel's wrongdoing, the two kingdoms fall to the Assyrian and Babylonian Empires. Jerusalem is destroyed, and the people are sent into exile.

THE WRITINGS

The Writings are placed after the historical books in the Christian Bible. Some of these are narratives covering the time of Israel's exile in other nations and its eventual return to the homeland. The Book of Esther, for example, tells the story of an unassuming Jewish girl who becomes the queen of Persia and boldly saves the Jewish people from genocide.

Many of the Writings are books of poetry and wisdom, among the most important literature in the Old Testament. The Book of Job is a lengthy dialogue investigating God's justice and the problem of human suffering. The Psalms are lyrical poems and hymns—many attributed to King David—that express humankind's longing for God. The books of Proverbs and Ecclesiastes—similarly attributed to the wise King Solomon—offer sayings and instructions about the meaning of life and ethical behavior. Lastly, the Song of Solomon (also attributed to Solomon) is a romantic, lyric dialogue between a young woman and her lover.

CHARACTER LIST

God   The creator of the world and an all-powerful being. God calls himself the only true deity worthy of human worship. As the figurehead of Israel and the force behind every event, God acts as the unseen hero of the Old Testament. God reveals his intentions by speaking to people. Physical manifestations of God are always indirect or symbolic. God appears in many different forms, including an angel, a wrestler, a burst of fire, and a quiet whisper.

Abraham   The patriarch of the Hebrew people. Abraham is traditionally called "Father Abraham" because the Israelite people and their religion descend from him. God establishes his covenant, or promise, with Abraham, and God develops an ongoing relationship with the Israelites through Abraham's descendants. Abraham practices the monotheistic worship of God, and his resilient faith in God, despite many challenges, sets the pattern for the Israelite religion's view of righteousness.

Moses   The reluctant savior of Israel in its exodus from Egyptian bondage to the promised land. Moses mediates between God and the people, transforming the Israelites from an oppressed ethnic group into a nation founded on religious laws. Moses's legendary miracles before Pharaoh, along with his doubts and insecurities, make him the great mortal hero of the Old Testament. He is the only man ever to know God "face to face." Four out of the five books of the Pentateuch are devoted to Moses and Israel's activities under his leadership.

David   The king of Israel and the founder of Jerusalem, or "Zion." David's reign marks the high point of Israel in the biblical narrative. Although David's claim to the throne is threatened by Saul and by David's own son, Absalom, David maintains his power by blending shrewd political maneuvering with a magnanimous and forgiving treatment of his enemies. David's decision to bring the Ark of the Covenant—Israel's symbol of God—to the capital of Jerusalem signals the long-awaited unification of the religious and political life of Israel in the promised land.

Jacob   The grandson of Abraham, Jacob is the third patriarch of the Israelite people and the father of the twelve sons who form the tribes of Israel. Jacob experiences a life fraught with deception, bewilderment, and change. He steals his brother Esau's inheritance right and wrestles with God on the banks of the Jabbok River. Appropriately, the nation that springs from Jacob's children derives its name from Jacob's God-given name, "Israel." "Israel" means "struggles with God," and Jacob's struggles are emblematic of the tumultuous story of the nation of Israel.

Joseph   Jacob's son and the head official for the Pharaoh of Egypt. Despite being sold into slavery by his brothers, Joseph rises to power in Egypt and saves his family from famine. Joseph's calm and gracious response to his brothers' betrayal introduces the pattern of forgiveness and redemption that characterizes the survival of the Israelite people throughout the Old Testament.

Saul   Israel's first king. After God chooses Saul to be king, Saul loses his divine right to rule Israel by committing two religious errors. Saul acts as a character foil to David, because his plot to murder David only highlights David's mercy to Saul in return. Saul's inner turmoil over the inscrutability of God's exacting standards makes him a sympathetic but tragic figure.

Solomon   David's son and the third king of Israel. Solomon builds the opulent Temple in Jerusalem and ushers in Israel's greatest period of wealth and power. God grants Solomon immense powers of knowledge and

discernment in response to Solomon's humble request
for wisdom. Solomon's earthly success hinders his
moral living, however, and his weakness for foreign
women and their deities leads to Israel's downfall.

Elijah & Elisha The prophets who oppose the worship of the
god Baal in Israel. After the division of Israel into two
kingdoms, Elijah and his successor, Elisha, represent
the last great spiritual heroes before Israel's exile. Their
campaign in northern Israel against King Ahab and
Jezebel helps to lessen Israel's growing evil but does
not restore Israel's greatness. Israel's demise makes
Elijah and Elisha frustrated doomsayers and miracle
workers rather than national leaders or saviors.

Adam & Eve The first man and woman created by God. Adam
and Eve introduce human evil into the world when
they eat the fruit of a tree God has forbidden them to
touch.

Noah The survivor of God's great flood. Noah obediently
builds the large ark, or boat, that saves the human race
and the animal kingdom from destruction. Noah is the
precursor to Abraham, because Noah represents the
first instance of God's attempt to form a covenant with
humanity through one person.

Isaac Abraham's son and the second member in the
triumvirate of Israel's patriarchs. Isaac's importance
consists less in his actions than in the way he is acted
upon by others. God tests Abraham by commanding
him to kill his son Isaac, and Isaac's blindness and
senility allow his own son Jacob to steal Isaac's
blessing and the inheritance of God's covenant.

Aaron Moses's brother, who assists Moses in leading the
Israelites out of Egypt. God designates Aaron to be the
first high priest in Israel. The quiet Aaron often stands
between Moses and the people to soften Moses's angry
response to their sinful behavior.

Joshua   The successor of Moses as Israel's leader. Joshua directs the people in their sweeping military campaign to conquer and settle the Promised Land. Joshua's persistent exhortations to Israel to remain obedient to God imply that he doubts Israel will do so. His exhortations foreshadow Israel's future religious struggles.

Samson   One of Israel's judges and an epic hero who thwarts the neighboring Philistines with his superhuman strength. Samson is rash, belligerent, and driven by lust for foreign women—qualities that contradict Jewish religious ideals. Samson's long hair is both the source of his strength and the symbol of his religious devotion to God as a Nazirite. Samson's character demonstrates that in the bible, heroic potential is gauged not by human excellence but by faith in God.

Samuel   The last of Israel's judges and the prophet who anoints both Saul and David as king. Samuel fulfills political and priestly duties for Israel, but he ushers in Israel's monarchy mainly as a prophet—one who pronounces God's words and decisions. Samuel's stoic and aloof position in Israel allows Saul to struggle with God and his fate on his own.

Absalom   David's son, who attempts to overthrow his father's throne. Absalom's violent rise to power suggests that the evil that corrupts Israel comes from within.

Joab   King David's loyal military commander. Joab serves as a foil to David's successful combination of religion and politics. Joab's reasonable desire to see justice and retribution delivered to the kingdom's traitors emphasizes the unusual quality of David's kindness to his enemies.

Rehoboam & Jeroboam   The opposing kings who divide Israel into the northern kingdom of Israel and the southern kingdom of Judah. Rehoboam and Jeroboam introduce rampant worship of idols and false gods into their kingdoms. Each king acts both as a point of contrast and a double, or mirror, for the other, allowing the biblical reader to trace the rapid growth of evil in Israel's two kingdoms.

Ahab & Jezebel The most wicked rulers of Israel. Ahab and Jezebel spread cult worship of the pagan god Baal throughout the northern kingdom. Dogs gather to eat their blood at their deaths, fulfilling Elijah's prophecy.

Esther A timid Jewish girl who becomes the queen of Persia. Esther boldly and cunningly persuades the king of Persia to remove his edict calling for the death of the exiled Jews.

Job The subject of God and Satan's cosmic experiment to measure human faithfulness to God in the midst of immense pain. Job scorns false contrition and the advice of his friends, preferring instead to question God's role in human suffering. He retains an open and inquisitive mind, remaining faithful in his refusal to curse God.

CHARACTER LIST

ANALYSIS OF MAJOR CHARACTERS

GOD

In the Old Testament, God is unique, sovereign, and unchanging. He differs from Greek gods, whose faults and quarrels cause events. His unchanging nature is hinted at by his names. In biblical Hebrew, God is called "YAHWEH," meaning "to be." This title is similar to the title God uses with Moses, "I AM WHO I AM." However, the God presented in Old Testament does contradict himself at times. In the course of two chapters in Exodus, God threatens to destroy the Israelites, relents, and then pronounces himself loving, forgiving, and slow to anger. God grants himself the power of self-description; he is whoever he says he is.

Each biblical writer gives God human characteristics. For example, God speaks. We do not know how his listeners recognize that it is he who is speaking or what he sounds like, but God certainly embraces the ability to articulate his intentions through the human convention of language. Also, God assumes human form. He appears as an angel, as a group of three men, and as a mysterious army commander. In a sense, God takes on human qualities like a costume that can also be taken off, since his specific appearances do not offer a complete picture of him. Still, these manifestations suggest that there is a fundamental humanity to the personality of the Hebrew God. God casually walks in the garden with Adam and Eve. He even physically wrestles Jacob and allows Jacob to beat him. These humble and endearing qualities of God contrast his later appearances as a pillar of fire and a thunderous mountain. The more extreme manifestations are, like the human manifestations, only a part of God's character rather than his sole mode of existence.

God's initial interaction with humankind is unsolicited. Noah, Abraham, and Moses do not ask God to form a relationship with them. Even when God is unseen, his immense power over human fate lurks beneath the events of the Old Testament narrative. On the surface, the characters' experiences are filled with suspense. The characters submit to chance and have a desperate, irrational faith in God. When God speaks or appears, we realize he has been in control all along, and the fear or suspense seems unfounded, trite, or comical. Amidst the gravity of human events, God's willingness to cause momentous events in order to teach a lesson shows him to be a strangely playful character.

MOSES

Moses is one of the few characters whose complete biography is described by the biblical narrative, and the early events of his life characterize him as a product of his circumstances. Born in Egypt, Moses is raised by Pharaoh's daughter, who takes pity on the abandoned Hebrew baby. After an impulsive murder, Moses flees west, where he begins a life as a shepherd and stumbles into God in the form of a burning bush. He reluctantly agrees to return to Egypt and demand the Israelites' release, but agrees to little more. Each event in the journey from Egypt to Mount Sinai, where God delivers his laws to the Israelites, propels Moses further into the roles of prophet, priest, ruler, and savior of Israel.

Moses' most heroic virtue is his steadfast obedience, and it might be said that a passive quality permeates each of his miracles. Ten plagues strike Egypt because Moses simply appears in Pharaoh's court to request the release of the Israelites. With the help of his rod, or divine staff, Moses parts the waters of the Red Sea merely by outstretching his arms. Later, the beleaguered Israelites defeat a mighty army when two men help Moses raise his hands for the duration of the battle. The image of a stationary man bringing about overwhelming physical feats is striking. Moses himself is far from passive or reticent, yet he represents a prototype of the biblical hero whose greatness lies not in self-assertion but in obedience to God.

Moses is a compelling figure because he possesses human faults. He is passionate and impulsive. Descending from Mount Sinai, Moses knows ahead of time that the people are worshipping a golden idol, because God has warned him of this fact. Upon seeing the people, Moses angrily breaks the stone tablets inscribed with God's laws. God seems to value this passionate quality in Moses, for Moses is an effective mediator between God and the Israelites. He prays with a sense of urgency, unafraid to ask God to refrain from divine retribution and willing to accept the blame for the people's actions. His earnest attention to the present situation and to God's demands earns Moses the opportunity to speak with God face to face. Yet his passion remains his weakness. God commands Moses to produce water from a rock by speaking to it, but, irritated with the people's complaints, Moses hits the rock with his staff. This act of negligence bars Moses from entering the very promised land to which he has guided the Israelites for almost half a century.

DAVID

CHARACTER ANALYSIS

David is a strong but unassuming shepherd who becomes God's choice to replace Saul as king of Israel. He is humble yet self-possessed, readily dismissing human opinion. His humility becomes clear early in his youth, when he kills the giant Goliath with a sling stone, declining the opportunity to use Saul's royal armor. As king, his foremost quality is obedience to God. For example, when his wife expresses embarrassment at David's dancing while he marches into Jerusalem, he rebukes her, boasting that he will embarrass himself so long as it pleases God.

David's mercy to others displays his selflessness—a product of his strenuous commitment to ethical ideals. His sense of propriety is striking when he refrains from killing Saul while Saul has his back turned. David scorns the easy opportunity to attack because he feels it would be morally wrong to strike God's current anointed ruler. As king, David forgives the kingdom's traitors, and executes the traitors of his enemies. When his own rebellious son dies, David cries aloud in public, "O my son Absalom, my son, my son Absalom!" (2 Samuel 18:33). His weeping suggests the depth of a father's blind love for his son.

David's mercy may also be interpreted as a product of his political aspirations. David refuses to kill Saul because he senses that whatever standards he imposes against the current king may one day be used against himself as ruler. Moreover, seeds of revolt have already been planted in the northern tribes of Israel by David's reign, and the kingdom's unity may be on shaky ground. King David shows mercy to his traitors, especially Absalom, because he wishes to quell emotions and court the graces of all his subjects. By this reading, David appears to be a pragmatist—one who acts not out of his or her ideals, but on the basis of what is practical or expedient. However, the Old Testament ultimately seems to suggest that David's religious ideals do not conflict with his pragmatism.

THEMES, MOTIFS & SYMBOLS

THEMES

Themes are the fundamental and often universal ideas explored in a literary work.

THE PROBLEM OF EVIL

The Old Testament both raises and attempts to answer the question of how God can be good and all-powerful yet allow evil to exist in the world. From Adam and Eve's first disobedient act in the garden, each biblical book affirms that human evil is the inevitable result of human disobedience, not of God's malice or neglect. The first chapters of Genesis depict God as disappointed or "grieved" by human wickedness, suggesting that the humans, rather than God, are responsible for human evil (Genesis 6:6). Later books, such as Judges and Kings, show God's repeated attempts to sway the Israelites from the effects of their evil. These stories emphasize the human capacity to reject God's help, implying that the responsibility for evil lies with humanity. Judges echoes with the ominous phrase, "The Israelites again did what was evil in the sight of the Lord . . ." (Judges 3:12).

The most troublesome challenge to God's goodness, however, is the existence of natural evil, which is the undeserved destruction and pain humans often experience. God repeatedly instructs the Israelites to destroy entire cities, killing men, women, and children in the process. The Book of Job directly questions God's implication in natural evil. God punishes Job harshly for no other reason than to prove to Satan that Job is religiously faithful. In the end, God declares to Job that God's powerful ways are beyond human understanding and should not be questioned. The book implies that God sometimes uses natural evil as a rhetorical device—as a means of displaying his power or of proving a point in a world already tainted by human corruption.

THE POSSIBILITY OF REDEMPTION

God typically responds to human behavior with retributive justice, meaning that people get what they deserve. God punishes the evil and blesses the righteous. The theme of mercy and redemption, which develops throughout the biblical stories, contrasts with this standard of retribution.

Redemption appears in two forms in the Old Testament. Sometimes, one person forgives another by simply forgetting or ignoring the other's offense. When Jacob returns to his homeland after cheating his brother, we expect hatred and vengeance from Esau. Instead, Esau welcomes Jacob with a joyful embrace, reversing Jacob's expectations no less than Jacob has already reversed Esau's fate. Similarly, King David treats his enemies with kindness and mercy, a policy that often seems shortsighted in its dismissal of traditional justice.

Another form of redemption involves the intervention of a third party as a mediator or sacrifice to quell God's anger with the wrongdoers. Moses's frantic prayers at Mount Sinai frequently cause God to "change his mind" and relent from destroying the Israelites (Exodus 32:14). In the Book of Judges, Samson sacrifices his life to redeem the Israelites from the Philistine oppression brought on by Israel's incessant evil. These human acts of redemption mirror God's promise in the religious laws to forgive the people's sins on the basis of ritual animal sacrifices and offerings.

THE VIRTUE OF FAITH

In the Old Testament, faith is a resilient belief in the one true God and an unshakable obedience to his will. The models of biblical faith are not those who are supported by organized religion but those who choose to trust in God at the most unpopular times. Part of the virtue of true faith is the ability to believe in God when he remains unseen. The Israelites betray their complete lack of faith when they complain after God repeatedly shows himself and displays miracles during the exodus from Egypt.

Noah, Abraham, and Elijah represent the three main heroes of faith in The Old Testament. Each demonstrates his faith in God by performing seemingly irrational tasks after God has been absent from humankind for an extended period of time. God has not spoken to humans for many generations when Noah obediently builds a large, strange boat in preparation for a monumental flood. Abraham similarly dismisses the idols and gods of his region in favor of a belief that an unseen and unnamed deity will provide

THEMES

a promised land for his descendants. Centuries later, the prophet Elijah attempts to rejuvenate faith in God after Israel has worshipped idols for decades. Like Noah and Abraham, Elijah develops a faith based on his ability to communicate directly with God.

MOTIFS

Motifs are recurring structures, contrasts, and literary devices that can help to develop and inform the text's major themes.

THE COVENANT

God's covenant with humankind incorporates both his promise to grant Abraham and Abraham's descendants a promised land and the religious laws given to the Israelites. The covenant resembles ancient legal codes and treaties in which a lord or landowner specifies the conditions of a vassal's service and vows to protect the vassal in return. The biblical covenant, however, represents not just a contractual agreement but also a passionate, tumultuous relationship between God and humanity. God's covenant passes to Abraham's descendants, unifying the lives of seemingly disparate people within a developing story. The biblical writers suggest that this story is not theirs but God's—a means for God to show his purposes and his values to humankind by relating to one family.

The covenant is a unifying structure that allows the human characters to evaluate their lives as a series of symbolic experiences. At first, the signs of the covenant are physical and external. God relates to Abraham by commanding Abraham to perform the rite of circumcision and to kill his son, Isaac. In Exodus, God shows his commitment to the Israelites by miraculously separating the waters of the Red Sea and appearing in a pillar of fire. The religious laws are also symbols of the covenant. They represent customs and behavioral rules that unite the lives of the Israelites in a religious community devoted to God. Moses suggests that these laws are to become sacred words that the Israelites cherish in their hearts and minds (Deuteronomy 11:18). The covenant thus shapes the personal memories and the collective identity of the Israelites.

DOUBLES AND OPPOSITES

At the beginning of Genesis, God creates the world by dividing it into a system of doubles—the sun and the moon, light and dark, the land and the sea, and male and female. When Adam and Eve eat the forbidden fruit, and when Cain kills his brother Abel, good and evil enter the world. From this point on, the Old Testament writers describe the world as a place of binary opposites, or sets of two basic opposing forces. These forces include positive and negative, good and bad, and lesser and greater. These distinctions characterize the ethics of the Israelites. The laws in Leviticus, Numbers, and Deuteronomy outline the criteria for being ceremonially clean or unclean, and for choosing obedience over disobedience.

Biblical writers frequently challenge these distinctions. As twins with opposing traits, Jacob and Esau represent ideal character doubles. When Jacob steals Esau's inheritance right, the younger son triumphs over the older son by dishonest, rather than honest, means. The reversal of fortune portrays God's covenant with humankind as a preference for the unexpected over the conventional, as well as God's willingness to accomplish his ends by imperfect means. The epic of Samson similarly blurs the line between weakness and strength. Samson, the icon of human strength, conquers the Philistines only after they bring him to his weakest by shaving his head and blinding him. Such stories question the human ability to tell the difference between good and bad.

GEOGRAPHY

The geography of the Old Testament determines the moral and religious well-being of the Hebrew people. The biblical authors circumscribe the spiritual story of Abraham and his descendants within a physical journey to and from the promised land. In a sense, the flow of the narrative can be summarized as a constant yearning for the promised land.

Displaced in Egypt, the Israelites grow in number without a religion or national identity. The journey with Moses to the promised land defines Israel's religion, laws, and customs. In Joshua, Judges, and the first book of Samuel, Israel's struggle to secure its borders mirrors its struggle to enjoy national unity and religious purity. David and Solomon's kingdoms represent the height of Israel, for Israel establishes a religious center in Jerusalem and begins to expand its territory. The division of the nation into northern and southern kingdoms represents the fragmentation of the promised land and, by implication, of God's promise to Israel. The ultimate exile into Assyria and Babylon denotes Israel's religious estrangement from God.

SYMBOLS

Symbols are objects, characters, figures, and colors used to represent abstract ideas or concepts.

THE FERTILE GROUND

The fertility of the earth symbolizes the quality of life of those who inhabit it. The garden paradise of Adam and Eve represents the ideal abundant existence for humanity. When God pronounces his curse to Adam, he curses the ground, vowing that humans will have to toil to produce food from the earth. God similarly destroys the ground when he sends the great flood. After Noah and his family emerge from the ark, however, the moist and fertile earth symbolizes the renewal of human life. When Joshua investigates the promised land in Numbers, he praises the region as a fruitful land that "flows with milk and honey" (Numbers 13:27). Biblical poetry frequently uses the image of fertile ground as a metaphor for human flourishing. In the Song of Solomon, a verdant, overgrown garden symbolizes the sexual maturity of a young woman. In Psalm 23, the psalmist emphasizes the herding culture of the ancient Hebrew people, characterizing God's peace as a shepherd who guides a sheep to green pastures.

THE ARK OF THE COVENANT

The Ark of the Covenant is Israel's chief symbol of God. The Israelites fashion the golden vessel at Mount Sinai according to God's instructions. The Ark contains a copy of the religious laws as well as a container of the heavenly food, manna. God's spirit or presence is said to reside between the two angels on the lid of the Ark in a space called "the mercy seat." The Ark's power is immense. When the Israelites carry it into the battle at Jericho, it ensures victory. When it is mistreated or dropped, or when it falls into the wrong hands, the Ark proves fatal to its handlers.

The Ark symbolizes the totality of all the symbols of God's covenant with the Israelites—it even represents God himself. As such, the Ark's location at each moment indicates Israel's commitment to the covenant. When the Ark does not have a permanent home or resting place, Israel's religious life remains disorganized. In the Book of Samuel, the Ark is actually stolen by the Philistines, representing a spiritual low-point for Israel. Israel's treatment of the Ark is thus emblematic of their reverence for God.

SUMMARY & ANALYSIS

GENESIS, CHAPTERS 1–11

SUMMARY

The Book of Genesis opens the Hebrew Bible with the story of creation. God, a spirit hovering over an empty, watery void, creates the world by speaking into the darkness and calling into being light, sky, land, vegetation, and living creatures over the course of six days. Each day, he pauses to pronounce his works "good" (1:4). On the sixth day, God declares his intention to make a being in his "own image," and he creates humankind (1:26). He fashions a man out of dust and forms a woman out of the man's rib. God places the two people, Adam and Eve, in the idyllic garden of Eden, encouraging them to procreate and to enjoy the created world fully, and forbidding them to eat from the tree of the knowledge of good and evil.

In the garden, Eve encounters a crafty serpent who convinces her to eat the tree's forbidden fruit, assuring her that she will not suffer if she does so. Eve shares the fruit with Adam, and the two are immediately filled with shame and remorse. While walking in the garden, God discovers their disobedience. After cursing the serpent, he turns and curses the couple. Eve, he says, will be cursed to suffer painful childbirth and must submit to her husband's authority. Adam is cursed to toil and work the ground for food. The two are subsequently banished from Eden.

Sent out into the world, Adam and Eve give birth to two sons, Cain and Abel. Cain, a farmer, offers God a portion of his crops one day as a sacrifice, only to learn that God is more pleased when Abel, a herdsman, presents God with the fattest portion of his flocks. Enraged, Cain kills his brother. God exiles Cain from his home to wander in the land east of Eden. Adam and Eve give birth to a third son, Seth. Through Seth and Cain, the human race begins to grow.

Ten generations pass, and humankind becomes more evil. God begins to lament his creation and makes plans to destroy humankind completely. However, one man, Noah, has earned God's favor because of his blameless behavior. God speaks to Noah and promises to establish a special covenant with Noah and his family. He instructs Noah to build an ark, or boat, large enough to hold Noah's family and pairs of every kind of living animal while God sends a great flood to destroy the earth. Noah does so, his family and the animals enter the ark, and rain falls in a deluge for forty days, submerging the earth in water for more than a year. When the waters finally recede, God calls Noah's family out of the ark and reaffirms his covenant with Noah. Upon exiting the ark, Noah's family finds that the earth is moist and green again. God promises that from this new fertile earth will follow an equally fertile lineage for Noah and his family. But humankind must follow certain rules to maintain this favor: humans must not eat meat with blood still in it, and anyone who murders another human must also be killed. God vows never to destroy the earth again, and he designates the rainbow to be a symbol of his covenant.

One night, Noah becomes drunk and lies naked in his tent. Ham, one of Noah's sons, sees his naked father and tells his brothers, Shem and Japeth. Shem and Japeth cover their father without looking at him. Upon waking, Noah curses Ham's descendants, the Canaanites, for Ham's indiscretion, declaring that they will serve the future descendants of Ham's brothers. A detailed genealogy of the three brothers' descendants is given. Many generations pass and humankind again becomes corrupt. Some men, having moved west to Babylon, attempt to assert their greatness and power by building a large tower that would enable them to reach the heavens. Their arrogance angers God, who destroys the edifice. He scatters the people across the earth by confusing their common language, thus forever dividing humankind into separate nations.

ANALYSIS

The first eleven chapters of Genesis tell an authoritative story about the beginnings of the world that contains many contradictions. Scholars believe that the account is not the work of one author, but of a later editor or "redactor" who collected stories from various traditional sources into one volume. For instance, the author of the story of Cain and Abel shows a knowledge of Jewish sacrificial law that only a later writer would possess. Also, the narrator's introduction of stories with phrases such as "This is the list of the descendants of Adam" (5:1) or "These are the descendants of Noah" (6:9) suggests these tales existed before the current writer or redactor collected them into their present form.

The major thematic link of the first eleven chapters is the structuring of the world around a system of parallels and contrasts. Light breaks into the darkness, land separates water, and "the greater light" of the sun opposes "the lesser light" of the moon (1:16). A more complex occurrence of parallel and contrast takes place with the account of man's creation. Man is not only made in the image of God, paralleling him, but woman, made from the man's rib, contrasts with man. The Genesis writer uses the poetic device of antistrophe, or the repetition of a line in reverse order, to highlight the parallels and contrasts in the creation of man:

> So God created humankind in his image,
> in the image of God he created them;
> male and female he created them.   1:27–29

The antistrophe suggests that the world is logically organized around binary opposites, or basic opposing forces. Positive and negative, work and rest, and day and night are among the many binary opposites that the first chapters of Genesis describe. Good and evil is probably the most consistently explored binary opposite in the Old Testament, and the story of Cain and Abel initiates a lengthy analysis of the difference between good and evil. Cain's deception and murder of Abel, as well as his evasive response to God's questioning, describe his evil as inherent in his character and unmitigated by other good traits. God's punishment, however, demonstrates both justice and mercy, establishing God as the absolute good that opposes Cain's absolute evil. God exiles Cain from God's presence, but marks Cain to protect him from the wrath of other people.

Images of the ground and of the earth recur in these chapters. In Genesis, mankind's relationship with the ground is often a measure of the quality and fullness of human life. God creates Adam from dust, and Adam's fate is connected to the earth when God curses him:

> cursed is the ground because of you;
> in toil you shall eat of it. . . .
> you are dust,
> and to dust you shall return.   3:17, 19

Cain is similarly cursed to the ground, for he is exiled from his home and sent to wander in a strange land. The ground is the object of God's rage when God sends the flood and, in some respects, when he destroys the Tower at Babel. However, the ground is also the symbol of God's blessing to Noah, for God's promise of fertility to Noah's family mirrors the green and plentiful quality of the earth.

In the account of Noah, God himself uses symbols as much as the authors of the story. God explicitly calls the rainbow a "sign," or symbol, of his covenant with humanity after the flood (9:12–13). God frequently uses physical objects to show his spiritual purposes. But unlike the Greek gods of Homer or other Near-Eastern deities, the Hebrew God is never depicted as limited or defined by these objects. Rather, the authors of Genesis suggest that God is telling an elaborate allegorical story through the act of creation and that as God manages the affairs of the earth, symbolic meaning is one of the primary ways in which he communicates with his creations.

The central purpose of these introductory chapters is to construct a detailed etiology, or explanation of the origins of the world. The author is trying to account for the way that certain unfavorable elements of everyday human life came into being. The etiological concerns are clear enough in these chapters. The writers and the redactors have collected stories that explain how evil and separate nations entered the world, why women must live in a society characterized by male standards, why we as humans must work to survive, and why our daily labor is always so hard.

GENESIS: CHAPTERS 12–25

> I will make you exceedingly fruitful; and I will make
> nations of you, and kings shall come from you.
>
> *(See* QUOTATIONS, *p. 76)*

SUMMARY

Nine generations of Shem's descendants, the Semites, pass. God calls on a man named Abram, living with his father Terah and his wife Sarai in Haran, a city in upper Mesopotamia. God makes a covenant with Abram, promising to make Abram's descendants into a great nation. Abram agrees to leave his home and move southwest to Canaan with his wife and his nephew, Lot, to a land that God has promised to give to Abram's descendants. Abram takes up residence there and erects a number of altars throughout the land as symbols of his devotion to God.

After a brief stay in Egypt, Abram becomes wealthy and returns to Canaan, where, with the help of only 318 men, he defeats a legion of marauding armies from the East that has descended upon Sodom, where Lot is currently living. The king of Sodom recognizes Abram for his great deed, and the priest Melchizedek blesses Abram with a gift of bread and wine. Abram returns home where God speaks to him again regarding his covenant. Abram's descendants, God promises, will be as numerous as the stars in the sky. A ceremony is performed in which God passes a blazing pot through pieces of sacrificed animals, symbolizing that his promise will not be broken. The writer notes that God considers Abram's faith in him as a form of righteousness.

Sarai cannot become pregnant, but she wants to give her husband an heir. To this end, she sends her handmaiden Hagar to sleep with Abram. When Sarai becomes upset because of Hagar's contempt, the handmaiden flees in fear. God speaks to Hagar and comforts her, promising her a son who will be a "wild ass of a man," and Hagar returns to give birth to Abram's first son, Ishmael (16:12). Once again, God speaks with Abram, this time enjoining Abram to remain blameless in his behavior and adding a new requirement to his everlasting covenant. Abram and all his descendants must now be circumcised as a symbol of the covenant, and God promises Abram a son through Sarai. The son is to be called Isaac, and it will be through Isaac that the covenant is fulfilled. God renames Abram "Abraham," meaning "father of many," and gives Sarai a new name, "Sarah."

One day, God appears to Abraham in the form of three men. The three men say that Sarah will have a son, but Sarah, who is now ninety years old, laughs. The three men travel toward the eastern cities of Sodom and Gomorrah to destroy the cities because of their flagrant wickedness and corruption. Abraham pleads on the cities' behalf, convincing the Lord not to destroy the cities if only a handful of good men can be found there. The men enter the city of Sodom, and Lot welcomes them into his home. Night falls, and the men of the city surround Lot's home, wishing to rape the three messengers. The messengers persuade Lot to flee the city with his family, telling him and his family not to look back as they leave. However, as God rains down burning sulfur on Sodom and Gomorrah, Lot's wife looks back at her home and is turned into a pillar of salt.

Abraham continues to gain political status in the area of Canaan, and Sarah eventually gives birth to Isaac. At Sarah's bidding, Abraham sends Hagar and Ishmael away. God again speaks to Abraham in a test, asking Abraham to kill his son, Isaac, as a sacrifice. Abraham quietly resolves to obey, and when he takes Isaac to the mountains, Isaac asks what animal they are going to sacrifice. Abraham replies that God will provide an offering. Isaac is laid on the altar, and just as Abraham is ready to strike, the angel of the Lord stops him. God is impressed with Abraham's great devotion and, once again, reaffirms his covenant.

Sarah dies. Abraham sends his chief servant to Abraham's relatives in Assyria to find a wife for Isaac, to prevent his lineage from being sullied by Canaanite influence. The servant prays to be guided to the correct wife for Isaac. God leads him to Rebekah, whom he brings back to Isaac. Isaac marries Rebekah, and Abraham dies soon thereafter.

ANALYSIS

This section contrasts with the earlier parts of Genesis by telling the extended story of one man, Abraham, and his family rather than combining stories, songs, and genealogies. Genesis traces Abraham's ancestry to Noah's son, Shem, in order to establish that Abraham is a member of both the Hebrew and Semitic peoples. Historically, tribes of nomadic people known as *habiru*—many of whom were Semitic—frequently moved among the ancient Canaanite cities; scholars believe that these nomads may be the roots of the Hebrew people. Whether or not Abraham was indeed the original ancestor of the Hebrew people is uncertain. But the story of Abraham is nevertheless significant to the religious tradition of faith and obedience it prescribes.

God's affirmation of his covenant with humankind now takes the form of an ongoing, personal relationship with a specific man and his descendants. The authors of Genesis describe God himself as a storyteller who uses the lives of the people who are obedient to him to describe a divine plot. God creates various symbols as reminders of the covenant, including the fiery pot at his second encounter with Abram, the custom of circumcision, and the renaming of Abram and Sarai. Poetic devices further emphasize the literary nature of the story and the importance of the covenant. God first verbalizes his covenant with Abram in the form of a song and later comforts Hagar in verse. These elements, especially the poetic, provide a break in the Genesis narrative, slowing down the plot and suggesting the grand, metaphysical significance of God's promise to Abraham.

These stories demonstrate the ways in which God gives dramatic rewards for absolute faith and obedience. At God's command, Abraham leaves his home to roam in a strange land; God's reward is to cause Abraham to discover great wealth. Sarah, barren her entire life, gives birth to a son at the age of ninety, an event so unlikely that she laughs when she is told that it will occur. And finally, Abraham receives God's greatest praise when he obediently stands poised to kill the very son through whom God has promised to fulfill his covenant. These moments depict absolute faith in God, despite the fact that his demands may seem illogical or unreasonable. What God consistently rewards is the abandonment of human reason and free will in favor of actions whose purpose is unknown or unknowable. As a result, these stories establish a version of God who knows what is best for mankind, but who reveals his purposes only selectively.

Another characteristic of the Old Testament God is the elusive manner in which he communicates with humans. Sometimes, people directly encounter God, as when God and Abraham converse. Frequently, however, God appears in the form of someone or something else, as when he visits Abraham in the form of three men. Throughout the Old Testament, God is alternately seen and unseen. Unlike the epics of the ancient Greeks, in which every event or action is described in full detail, there are always details in Genesis and the Hebrew Bible that remain unexplained because God so often insists on removing himself from the action. The most important instance of God's absence is when God tests Abraham. After requesting that Abraham sacrifice Isaac, God disappears without stating his true intentions, leaving Abraham to move forward in silence to the mountain where he will, supposedly, kill his son. In this story, God's absence serves the purpose of testing Abraham's faith in the infallibility of God, even when God does not explain his demands. Furthermore, the removal of God from the story greatly increases the drama and suspense of the Genesis narrative.

GENESIS CHAPTERS 25–50

SUMMARY

Following Abraham's death, God reveals to Isaac's wife Rebekah that she will soon give birth to two sons who will represent two nations, one stronger than the other. When Rebekah delivers, Esau is born first and is extremely hairy. Jacob, who is smooth skinned, is born immediately after, grasping the heel of his brother. Isaac's two sons grow to be opposites. Esau is a hunter and a brash man. Jacob stays at home, soft-spoken but quick-witted. One day, Esau comes home famished, demanding to be fed, and agrees to give Jacob his inheritance rights in exchange for a bowl of soup.

Like his own father, Isaac prospers in Canaan and, despite occasional errors in judgment, enlarges his property, making alliances

SUMMARY & ANALYSIS

THE OLD TESTAMENT ❦ 29

with area rulers and continuing to erect monuments to God. One day, when he is old and blind, Isaac instructs Esau to catch some game and prepare him a meal so that he may give the elder son his blessing. While Esau is gone, Rebekah helps Jacob deceive his father, preparing a separate meal and disguising the younger son with hairy arms and Esau's clothing. When Jacob presents Isaac with the meal, Isaac—smelling Esau's clothing and feeling the hairy body—proceeds to bless Jacob, promising him the inheritance of God's covenant and a greater status than his brother. Esau returns to discover the deception, but it is too late. Isaac, though dismayed, says that he cannot revoke the stolen blessing.

Jacob flees in fear of Esau, traveling to the house of his uncle Laban in upper Mesopotamia. En route, Jacob dreams of a stairway leading up to heaven, where angels and God reside. In the dream, God promises Jacob the same covenant he previously made with Abraham and Isaac. Jacob arrives at Laban's house, where he agrees to work for his uncle in exchange for the hand of Laban's daughter, Rachel, in marriage. Laban deceives Jacob into marrying Leah, Rachel's older sister, before marrying Rachel. The two wives compete for Jacob's favor and, along with their maids, give birth to eleven sons and a daughter.

After twenty years, Jacob heeds God's urging and leaves to return to Canaan, taking his family, his flocks, and Laban's collection of idols, or miniature representations of gods. Rachel, who has stolen the idolic figurines from her father, hides them under her skirt when Laban tracks down the fleeing clan in the desert. Unable to procure his belongings, Laban settles his differences with Jacob, who erects a pillar of stone as a "witness" to God of their peaceful resolution (31:48). Jacob continues on and, nearing home, fears an encounter with Esau. Jacob prepares gifts to appease his brother and, dividing his family and belongings into two camps, spends the night alone on the river Jabbok. Jacob meets God, who, disguised as a man, physically wrestles with Jacob until dawn. Jacob demands a blessing from his opponent, and the man blesses Jacob by renaming him "Israel," meaning, "he struggles with God."

The next morning, Jacob meets Esau, who welcomes his brother with open arms. Jacob resettles in Shechem, not far from Esau, who has intermarried with the Canaanites and produced a tribe called the Edomites. Jacob and his sons prosper in peace until one day Jacob's daughter, Dinah, is raped by a man from Shechem. Enraged, Jacob's sons say they will let the Shechemite marry Dinah if all the members of the man's family will be circumcised. The man agrees and, while the greater part of his village is healing from the surgical procedure, Jacob's sons take revenge and attack the Shechemites, killing all the men. Isaac and Rachel die soon thereafter.

Jacob's sons grow jealous of their youngest brother, Joseph, who is Jacob's favorite son. When Jacob presents Joseph with a beautiful, multi-colored coat, the eleven elder brothers sell Joseph into slavery, telling their father that Joseph is dead. Joseph is sold to Potiphar, a high-ranking official in Egypt, who favors the boy greatly until, one day, Potiphar's flirtatious wife accuses Joseph of trying to sleep with her. Potiphar throws Joseph in prison, but—ever faithful to God—Joseph earns a reputation as an interpreter of dreams. Years pass until the Pharaoh of Egypt, bothered by two troublesome dreams, hears of Joseph and his abilities. Pharaoh summons Joseph, who successfully interprets the dreams, warning Pharaoh that a great famine will strike Egypt after seven years. Impressed, Pharaoh elects Joseph to be his highest official, and Joseph leads a campaign throughout Egypt to set aside food in preparation for the famine.

Famine eventually plagues the land and, learning of the Egyptian supply of grain, Joseph's brothers go to Egypt to purchase food. The eleven men present themselves to Joseph, who recognizes them immediately but refrains from revealing his identity. Joseph toys with his brothers to test their good will, first throwing them in jail and then sending them back to Canaan to retrieve their newest brother, Benjamin. They return with the boy, and Joseph continues his game, planting a silver cup in the boy's satchel and threatening to kill the boy when the cup is discovered. When Judah offers his own life in exchange for Benjamin's, Joseph reveals his identity. Joseph persuades his brothers to return to Egypt with Jacob, who, overjoyed, moves to Egypt with his family of seventy.

As Jacob approaches death, he promises Joseph that the covenant will pass on through Joseph and his two sons, Manasseh and Ephraim. However, when Jacob places his hands on the two boys to bless them, he crosses his arms, placing his right hand on Ephraim, the younger son. Joseph protests, but Jacob says that Ephraim will be greater than Manasseh. Jacob dies soon thereafter and, accompanied by Egyptians, Joseph buries his father in Canaan. They return to Egypt, where Jacob's descendants, the Israelite people, grow rapidly. Joseph eventually dies, instructing his family to return one day to the land God has promised to give to Abraham, Isaac, and Jacob.

ANALYSIS

The division of the world into binary opposites, initiated with the creation story, dominates the latter half of Genesis. Just as light absolutely opposes darkness and male absolutely opposes female in the creation story, Esau and Jacob are diametrically opposed in everything from their appearance to their occupations and behavior. Rachel and Leah constitute another pair of binary opposites, struggling with each other for Jacob's affections. Oppositions continue, not only between Joseph's sons, Ephraim and Mannasseh, but with other, more intangible elements, such as the wrestling match between God and man, the contrast between abundance and famine in Egypt, and the decidedly joyful welcome of Esau after Jacob's expectations of a violent homecoming. Alongside the motif of opposites runs a motif of substitution or crossing; Jacob is blessed instead of Esau, and Jacob himself crosses his arms when he blesses Joseph's sons, bestowing the higher blessing on the younger son.

These opposing elements generate both irony and radical reversals in the stories of Isaac, Jacob, and Joseph. Esau does not merely receive a lesser blessing because Jacob steals his inheritance but is actually cursed to serve his younger brother forever, barred from the covenant entirely. Characters are increasingly tricky or deceptive in these stories, and their skill at deception usually earns them praise and privilege rather than punishment. Jacob deceives Esau, and as a result becomes the founder of one of the greatest nations in the Old Testament. Laban deceives Jacob, and receives twice as many years of service from him as a result. Rachel hides her father's idols under her dress, and Jacob's sons murderously trick the Shechemites. The most interesting deception, on a literary level, is Joseph's decision to veil his identity from his brothers. The elaborate deception builds in suspense over four chapters, as the narrative does not make it clear whether Joseph plans to enact revenge or simply to scare his brothers. When Judah offers to give his life for Benjamin, and Joseph forgives his brothers, trickery is replaced by the possibility of redemption, foreshadowing God's plan to reverse the Israelites' fortune with a promise of abundance in a new land.

Joseph plays a game of punishment and redemption with his brothers, and God plays the same game with the whole of humanity throughout Genesis. God creates a realm of opposing forces, symbols, and reversals to suggest a pattern of how and through whom his covenant will be revealed. The game is in the foreground, while

God and his reasons for playing the game move into the background of the Genesis narrative. The game becomes literal rather than figurative when God wrestles Jacob by the Jabbok River. The event is a metaphor for how God conveys his promise to humankind in the second half of Genesis. Just as the mysterious man never identifies himself to Jacob, so God recedes further and further from humankind. Jacob, however, is able to see past his opponent's bodily appearance because he is persistent and faithful, eventually able to wrest a blessing from this obscured manifestation of God. The giving of the name "Israel" to Jacob not only commemorates this specific struggle but also commemorates the struggle of the Israelites with an unseen God. Joseph, the ancestor of the Israelites, never has an explicit conversation with God, yet he notes in the final chapter of Genesis that the happy outcome of the first trick his brothers play on him has helped to save many lives in Egypt. The experience of Joseph and Jacob shows that God's covenant is fulfilled largely through the act of struggling.

Exodus

Summary

The Book of Exodus begins more than four hundred years after Joseph, his brothers, and the Pharaoh he once served have all died. The new leadership in Egypt—feeling threatened by Jacob's descendants, who have increased greatly in size—embarks on a campaign to subdue the Israelites, forcing them into slavery and eventually decreeing that all Hebrew boys must be killed at birth in the Nile River. The Hebrew women resist the decree, and one woman opts to save her newborn son by setting him afloat on the river in a papyrus basket. Fortunately, Pharaoh's daughter discovers the abandoned child and raises him after he has been nursed, naming him Moses.

Moses is aware of his Hebrew roots, and, one day, he kills an Egyptian who is beating an Israelite worker. Moses flees in fear to Midian, a town near Sinai, where he meets a priest named Jethro and marries the man's daughter, beginning a new life as a shepherd. God, however, is concerned for the suffering of the Israelites, and he appears to Moses in the form of a burning bush. God speaks to Moses, informing him of his plan to return the Israelites to Canaan—to "a land flowing with milk and honey" (3:8)—and to send Moses back to Egypt to accomplish this task. Moses is timid and resists, citing his lack of eloquence and abilities, and refuses to go. God is angered but encourages Moses, presenting him with a staff for performing miracles and instructing Moses to take his brother, Aaron, with him as an aid. When Moses asks God what his name is, God replies, "I AM WHO I AM" (3:14).

Moses and Aaron return to Egypt, where Moses organizes the Israelites and confronts the Pharaoh, demanding the release of the Hebrew people. Moses performs a miracle, turning his staff into a snake, but Pharaoh is unimpressed and only increases the workload for the Israelites. God responds by inflicting a series of ten plagues on Egypt. God turns the Nile River into blood, causes frogs to cover Egypt, turns all of the dust in Egypt to gnats, and causes swarms of flies to come into the houses of Pharaoh and his officials. God then strikes Egypt's livestock with a disease, creates festering boils on humans and animals, and sends thunder, hail, and fire that destroy crops, livestock, and people. God sends swarms of locusts, and covers Egypt with "a darkness that can be felt" (10:21). Before each plague, Moses demands the Israelites' release, and after each plague, God purposefully "hardens" Pharaoh so that he refuses the request (4:21, 7:22). The tenth and final plague kills all the firstborn males in Egypt. Before the plague, Moses instructs the Hebrew people to cover their door posts in the blood of a sacrificed lamb as a sign for God to protect their homes from his killings. Pharaoh relents and releases the more than 600,000 Israelites who, in turn, plunder the Egyptians' wealth. Upon leaving, Moses enjoins the Israelites to commemorate this day forever by dedicating their firstborn children to God and by celebrating the festival of Passover, named for God's protection from the final plague (12:14–43).

Guided by a pillar of cloud during the day and by fire during the night, Moses and the Israelites head west toward the sea. Pharaoh chases them. The Israelites complain that Moses has taken them to die in the wilderness, and Moses, at God's bidding, parts the sea for the people to cross. Pharaoh follows and Moses closes the waters back again, drowning the Egyptian army. Witnessing the miracle, the people decide to trust Moses, and they sing a song extolling God as a great but loving warrior. Their optimism is brief, and the people soon begin to worry about the shortage of food and water. God responds by sending the people food from heaven, providing a daily supply of quail and a sweet bread-like substance called manna. The people are required only to obey God's commandments to enjoy this food. Soon thereafter, the Israelites confront the warring Amalekite people, and God gives the Israelites the power to defeat them. During battle, whenever Moses raises his arms, the Israelites are able to rout their opponents.

Three months after the flight from Egypt, Moses and the Israelites arrive at Mount Sinai, where God appears before them, descending on the mountain in a cloud of thunder and lightning. Moses climbs the mountain, and God gives Moses two stone tablets with ten commandments inscribed on them regarding general, ethical behavior as well as an extended series of laws regarding worship, sacrifices, social justice, and personal property. God explains to Moses that if the people will obey these regulations, he will keep his covenant with Israel and will go with them to retrieve from the Canaanites the land promised to Abraham. Moses descends from the mountain and relates God's commandments to the people. The people agree to obey, and Moses sprinkles the people with blood as a sign of the covenant. Moses ascends to the mountain again where God gives him more instructions, this time specifying in great detail how to build a portable temple called an ark in which God's presence will dwell among the Israelites. God also emphasizes the importance of observing the Sabbath day of holy rest.

Moses comes down from the mountain after forty days, only to find that Aaron and the Israelites have now erected an idol— a golden calf that they are worshipping in revelry, in direct defiance of the ten commandments. Moses breaks the stone tablets on which God has inscribed the new laws, and God plans to destroy the people. Moses intercedes on the Israelites' behalf, begging God to relent and to remember his covenant. Pleased with Moses, God is appeased and continues to meet with Moses face to face, "as one speaks to a friend," in a special tent set aside for worship (33:11). God reaffirms his covenant with Moses, and, fashioning new stone tablets to record his decrees, God declares himself to be a compassionate, loving, and patient God. At Moses's direction, the Israelites renew their commitment to the covenant by erecting a tabernacle to God according to the exact specifications God has outlined.

ANALYSIS

While Genesis explains the origins of the world and of humanity, Exodus is the theological foundation of the Bible. Exodus explains the origins of Torah—the law of the Jewish people and the tradition surrounding that law. Torah is not merely a list of laws, but, rather, the notion of law as a way of life. Indeed, the law exists as a way of life for Moses and his people. Although portions of Exodus are devoted to legal matters, the declaration of law in Exodus always comes in the form of a story, relayed by discussions between God and Moses, and between Moses and the people.

These laws and tradition are filled with symbols of God's promise to the Israelites. In Genesis, God uses symbols such as the rainbow and gives people new names, like Abraham, as signs of his covenant. Such personalized signs are useful when communicating a promise to a single person or family. In Exodus, however, God attempts to communicate his promise to an entire nation of people. Social laws about how the Israelites should treat their slaves and annual festivals such as Passover are signs that a community of people can easily recognize and share. In this sense, obedience to God's laws is less a means of achieving a level of goodness than it is a way for the people to denote their commitment to God's covenant.

The Hebrew word for "Exodus" originally means "names," and Exodus is often called the Book of Names. The book discusses the different names God takes and the various ways God manifests himself to the Israelites. When God tells Moses that his name is "I AM" (3:14), God defines himself as a verb (in Hebrew, *ahyh*) rather than a noun. This cryptic statement suggests that God is a being who is not subject to the limits of people's expectations or definitions. Most often, however, God reveals himself to the people through theophany: extraordinary natural phenomena that signal God's arrival or presence. Theophanic events in Exodus include the pillars of cloud and fire, the thunder at Mount Sinai, and the miraculous daily supply of manna. Such spectacles demonstrate God's attempts to prove his existence to a nation of doubting people from whom he has been decidedly absent for more than four hundred years. The unwillingness of the people to accept God's existence is never more apparent than when the Israelites worship a golden calf in the shadow of the thunderous Mount Sinai. As a result, God's final manifestation of himself is the tabernacle—specifically, the Ark of the Covenant, a golden vessel in which God's presence, or spirit, will reside. Like the law, the Ark is an effective symbol of God, for it is an object that the people not only build as a community according to God's specifications but also as a religious vessel that can be picked up and carried wherever Israel goes.

Moses is the first true hero we encounter in the Hebrew Bible. He manifests all the traits of a traditional hero. He overcomes timidity and inner strife. He challenges Pharaoh, leading Israel to great feats. And he wields his own weapon, the miraculous staff. These elements give Moses traditional heroic status, but Moses also presents us with a new type of hero—the religious priest. All of Moses's political and military dealings serve the one end of delivering the Israelites to God, physically moving them from Egypt to Mount Sinai and interceding to God for them when they disobey. As God declares early on, Moses is God's representative to the people, and Moses makes God's relationship with Israel a personal one. Instead of a series of incendiary explosions, Moses presents God's instructions to the people through conversation and conveys God's desire to destroy the Israelites by breaking the stone tablets in front of them. Most importantly, Moses's dialogue with God enables the author to portray God in softer, human terms—as someone who listens, grieves, and is actually capable of changing his mind.

LEVITICUS, NUMBERS & DEUTERONOMY

You shall love the Lord your God with all your heart,
and with all your soul, and with all your might.

(See QUOTATIONS, *p. 77*)

SUMMARY

Throughout Leviticus, Israel remains encamped at Mount Sinai while God appears in the Tent of Meeting, dictating to Moses his specifications regarding the Jewish ceremonial laws. The laws are extremely detailed, outlining every aspect of how and when religious offerings are to be presented to God. God gives the instructions himself, and his voice comprises the majority of the text. A brief narrative interlude describes the anointing of Aaron and his sons as Israel's priests. At the ceremony, God appears and engulfs the altar in a burst of flames, eliciting shouts of joy from the people. Soon after, God also sends fire to consume two of Aaron's sons when they neglect to make the right preparations for approaching the altar.

God lists various types of forbidden sexual behavior and discusses foods and physical conditions that can make a person unclean. Uncleanliness can result from things such as bodily discharge or touching a dead carcass. An unclean person must leave the Israelite camp or undergo physical cleansing, waiting periods, and religious sacrifices. Typically, sexual sins are punishable by death, but God also instructs the Israelites to kill a man who blasphemes, or curses God's name. Of all his restrictions, God places particular emphasis on the prohibition against eating meat with blood still in it: doing so will result in banishment, not only from Israel but from God's graces as well.

SUMMARY & ANALYSIS

In the end, God promises to give Israel great abundance and success if it obeys these laws. If Israel is disobedient, though, God will send destruction and famine and "abhor" the Israelites (26:30). But the laws in Leviticus also set aside an annual Day of Atonement during which the priest is to offer sacrifices for the forgiveness of the entire nation. As long as the Israelites confess and repent for their sins, God promises to keep his covenant and never leave them.

At the beginning of Numbers, Israel prepares to continue the journey from Mount Sinai to the promised land. God devotes one of the twelve tribes, the Levites, to assist Aaron in the work of the priesthood, maintaining and watching over Israel's religious articles. After dedicating the Tabernacle, which houses the Ark of the Covenant, the Israelites leave Sinai, guided by the movements of a cloud that rests over the Tabernacle. Entering the desert, the people begin to complain about everything from the lack of interesting food to Moses's leadership.

Moses sends spies into Canaan to explore the promised land. Upon returning, two of the spies, Joshua and Caleb, report that Israel can successfully conquer the Canaanite people with God's help. However, some of the spies incite an uprising, arguing that it will be impossible to take the land from the Canaanites and that Israel should return to Egypt instead. God plans to destroy the people for their lack of faith, but Moses intervenes and convinces God to forgive them. God relents but delivers a heavy curse. He announces that the current generation of Israelites, with the exception of Joshua and Caleb, will not be allowed to enter the promised land. Moses leads the people back toward the Red Sea to wander in the wilderness for a period of forty years.

Another revolt occurs when three men grow jealous of Moses's leadership. God plans to destroy the entire nation because of the men's jealousy, but Moses persuades God to destroy only the guilty parties. Moses warns the people that the men will die as a result of their own disobedience. God causes the ground to open and swallow the men, but the Israelites blame Moses and Aaron for the incident. Very angry, God sends a rapidly spreading plague through the crowd, killing thousands. Aaron runs out into the crowd and holds up the priest's censer to atone for Israel's wrongdoing, stopping the plague in its destructive path.

Following this event, Moses and Aaron themselves disobey God. The people continue to complain about the lack of water and express their longing to be back in Egypt. God instructs Moses to speak to a rock and command it to produce water. Moses, instead, hits the rock angrily with his staff. The rock proceeds to pour forth water, but God tells Moses and Aaron that they, too, will never enter the promised land because of this brash act. Aaron dies soon after, and the priesthood passes on to Aaron's son Eleazar.

Israel wanders in the lands southwest of Canaan, requesting safe passage from the surrounding nations but receiving little hospitality in return. With God's help, Israel conquers the Amorites and settles in their lands. Learning of the overthrow, the king of Moab summons a renowned sorcerer, Balaam, to come and pronounce a curse on the Israelites. The angel of God intercepts Balaam on the road to Moab, frightening Balaam's donkey. When Balaam strikes the panicked animal, the donkey miraculously speaks, rebuking Balaam. The Lord points out the angel's presence. The angel of God forbids Balaam to curse the Israelites before the king of Moab. Balaam arrives in Moab and delivers four cryptic oracles to the king, blessing Israel and predicting Moab's destruction.

The Israelite men succumb to the surrounding native peoples by fraternizing with the local women and worshipping the pagan god Baal. God sends a plague on Israel that ends only when Eleazar's son, the priest, kills an Israelite man and his Midianite mistress, stabbing them before all of Israel with a single thrust of his spear. Eleazar's son's impassioned act earns God's approval, and God leads Israel in destroying the Midianites, plundering their wealth in the process. As the forty-year waiting period draws to a close, God appoints Joshua to eventually succeed Moses as the people's leader.

The Book of Deuteronomy begins in the final, fortieth year of Israel's wandering in the desert. Stationed east of the Jordan River, Moses addresses the new generation of Israelites in preparation for entering the promised land. He summarizes the events of the past four decades and encourages the young Israelites to remember God's miracles and covenant with Israel. He forbids the worship of other gods or idols in the new land and repeats the Ten Commandments given by God at Mount Sinai. Most importantly, Moses gives explicit instructions to the Israelites to destroy all the native inhabitants of the promised land so that the Canaanites do not interfere with Israel's worship of God. Moses restates many of the social laws and rules of conduct outlined in Leviticus, adding a few new laws, such as the requirement for the Israelites to cancel debts every seven years.

Moses stresses God's love for Israel, describing God as someone who protects orphans, widows, and oppressed people. Israel is to love God intensely in return, with absolute devotion. The words of God's laws are very important. Moses instructs the Israelites to meditate on these words and to write the laws on their bodies and on the doorframes of their homes. Moses argues that the love of God and a commitment to his laws will be considered goodness for Israel (6:25). While Moses predicts that Israel will eventually grow disobedient, he notes that God will welcome Israel back with abundance and prosperity whenever Israel returns to obedience.

At God's direction, Moses composes a song that recounts Israel's history of unfaithfulness and extols God's everlasting compassion. Moses says the song will be a reminder to future Israelites of their covenant with God. He writes the song in the Book of the Laws and places the book with the Ark of the Covenant. Afterward, Moses ascends a mountain where God shows him a vision of the promised land. Moses dies and is buried by God. The author praises him as the only prophet in Israel's history who performed such impressive miracles and who knew God "face to face" (34:10).

ANALYSIS

The books of Leviticus, Numbers, and Deuteronomy form the bulk of the Hebrew law, or Torah. Each text mixes procedural instructions and legal matters with a variety of narrative voices and action. The separate books are probably the collected writings of priests with different interests and perspectives, written sometime during Israel's tumultuous exile in the seventh and sixth centuries B.C. The three works document an important stage in the development of Israel's identity as a people and a nation. The prose is frequently arduous and repetitive, but it functions as a long, concentrated pause in the narrative of the Old Testament. Israel's wandering in the desert can be seen as the nation's adolescence—a period of education and growth following the nation's birth in the exodus from Egypt and the events at Mount Sinai.

The fact that the Israelites' punishment for certain infractions is to isolate or expel the offending individual from the camp demonstrates the extraordinary desire of the people to remain part of the community. The Israelite camp is set up in concentric circles with the tabernacle at its center: Moses and Aaron are closest to the tabernacle, followed by the Levites who care for it, and the rest of the tribes surround them. Since uncleanness bars a person from approaching the sacred religious items, physical impurity places one farthest from the center of Israel. In this way, God's injunctions challenge the

Israelites to strive to remain near the nation's center. The distinction between purity and impurity helps promote a distinction between an accepted, privileged "us" and an outcast "them" who are outside the circle of the community.

Moses's emphasis on the word "heart" in his sermons is also critical to Israel's understanding of itself as a unified people. Moses describes the physical and external regulations of the law by using spiritual and internal imagery. He says, "Hear, O Israel: The Lord is our God, the Lord alone. You shall love the Lord your God with all your heart, and with all your soul, and with all your might. Keep these words that I am commanding you today in your heart" (Deuteronomy 6:6). The idea that Israel as a whole has a "heart" or a group of "hearts" suggests that the nation has developed a set of personal or private experiences over the forty years of wandering in the desert. This waiting period distances Israel from Egypt and the laws at Mount Sinai, forcing the nation to form a collective memory of these events. When Moses instructs the people, "You shall put these words of mine in your heart and soul," he encourages them to internalize and embrace these collective, national memories (Deuteronomy 11:18). Moses portrays the religious laws no longer as a list of actions to be performed in the future but as sacred words and ideas that are a part of a past and an internal life that is unique to Israel.

The description of God as loving and compassionate in Deuteronomy is perplexing in light of God's intense wrath in Numbers. Moses, however, seems to see God's violent reaction to Israel's complaints and infidelities as an exercise or a test of Israel's commitment to the covenant. Indeed, God's destruction follows a consistent pattern in Numbers: the people complain and wish to return to Egypt; God threatens to destroy the people; Moses or another representative intercedes on behalf of the people; and God relents, punishing only a portion of Israel's population. The climax in these exercises occurs when representatives of the people speak on behalf of Israel. The moment of intercession when the plague is stopped by Aaron running into the crowd or by Eleazar's son stabbing the man and his foreign mistress are both climactic. Man's intercession does not require God to stop his destruction, but it creates the opportunity for Israel's leaders to display religious zeal and for God to show his mercy. God manifests his compassion and love not by what he does, but by what he does not do. Israel emerges from these encounters as a nation that has survived trials and hardship—a resilient people, with its weakest members now weeded out.

JOSHUA

SUMMARY

After the death of Moses, God calls on Joshua to lead the Israelites across the Jordan River and take possession of the promised land. God guarantees victory in the military campaign and vows never to leave the Israelites so long as they obey his laws. The people swear their allegiance to Joshua, and he sends two spies across the river to investigate the territory. The men enter Jericho, where a prostitute named Rahab hides them in her home and lies to the city officials regarding the spies' presence. Rahab tells the spies that the Canaanites are afraid of Israel and its miraculous successes. Professing belief in the God of the Israelites, she asks for protection for her family when the Israelites destroy Jericho. The spies pledge to preserve Rahab and return to Joshua, telling him of the weakened condition of Israel's enemies.

The Israelites cross the Jordan River, led by a team of priests carrying the Ark of the Covenant. As the priests enter the water, the flow of the river stops and the Israelites cross the river on dry land. Arriving on the other side, the Israelites commemorate the miracle with an altar of twelve stones from the river bed (representing the twelve tribes of Israel). The people begin to eat the produce of the new land—thus halting the daily supply of manna—and the Israelite men perform the ritual of circumcision in preparation for battle.

Approaching Jericho, Joshua encounters a mysterious man who explains that he is the commander of God's army but that he is neither for nor against Israel. Joshua pays homage to the man and passes on. Following divine instructions, Joshua leads the Israelites in carrying the Ark around Jericho for six days. On the seventh day, the Israelites march around the city seven times. Joshua rallies them to conquer the city and kill everyone except for Rahab. They are to refrain from taking any of the city's religious items. At the sound of the Israelite war cry, the walls of Jericho collapse, and the Israelites destroy the city and its inhabitants.

Joshua's fame spreads throughout the land, but the Israelites are humiliated in their attempts to take the next city, Ai. God attributes the disaster to the disobedience of Achan, an Israelite who has stolen religious items from Jericho. After the people stone Achan, the renewed attempt against Ai is successful as Joshua masterminds an elaborate ambush against the city's forces. The Israelites celebrate by erecting an altar to God and publicly reaffirming their commitment to God's law.

Fearful of the marauding Israelites, the people of Gibeon visit the Israelite camp in disguise, claiming to be travelers in the land and requesting peace with Israel. Joshua does not inquire with God and makes a hasty treaty with the men, only to discover later that the Gibeonites are natives of the land to be conquered. The Israelites refrain from attacking the city, but five other local kings attack Gibeon for making peace with Israel. The Israelites come to Gibeon's aid and destroy the five armies. Joshua helps by commanding God to make the sun stand still during the fight. God listens and stops the sun's movement—the only time in history, we are told, when God obeys a human.

The Israelites continue to destroy the southern and northern cities of Canaan, killing all living inhabitants, as God has stipulated. While much of the promised land still remains to be conquered, the people of Israel begin to settle in the land, dividing it amongst the twelve tribes. After God gives Israel rest from its enemies for many years, an ailing Joshua makes a farewell pronouncement to the nation of Israel. Joshua goads the Israelites to be strong and to obey all of God's laws, throwing away any idols and refraining from intermarriage with the native people. The people assure Joshua they will be faithful to the covenant, but Joshua reluctantly accepts this assurance, worried that obedience for Israel will prove quite difficult.

ANALYSIS

Scholars dispute the historical accuracy of the Book of Joshua. Although the writer claims to be writing in the thirteenth century B.C., it is unlikely that Joshua was written that early, and it is unlikely that the conquest of Palestine by the Hebrew people was as clean and neat as the first twelve chapters of Joshua suggest. Some scholars choose to read the book not as an inaccurate record of history but as an accurate record of Hebrew cultural memory of the original invasion of Palestine by the wandering Israelites. Unlike Genesis and Exodus, Joshua contains detailed accounts of political and military battles, and more than half of the book is devoted to listing the allotment of land to each of the twelve tribes. Few of the characters are as dramatic as those in the first books of the Old Testament, and God interferes little with human lives. In this sense, Joshua reads more like an ancient Hebrew history textbook than a collection of separate myths and legends.

The Book of Joshua carefully structures its description of the invasion of Palestine. The strict organization of the book emphasizes that the description of the conquests is a literary interpretation, and shows the importance within this interpretation of the idea of land. Israel's conquest is divided into two parts: the first twelve chapters tell the story of the conquest itself, and the final twelve chapters tell the story of how the land was allotted. These two sections are each subdivided into two sections. In these four parts, Israel prepares for the conquest, the campaigns themselves are carried out, the conquered land is allotted, and a concluding section exhorts Israel to remain loyal to God. The geographic organization of the book is equally rigorous; both the conquests and the division of lands are grouped according to whether the lands are in the north, south, east, or west. In the process, the idea of land plays a role as antagonistic as any character's. Various people's desire for and loyalty to specific regions is a source of great conflict, and God's covenant with Israel is physically manifested in his promise of land.

The Book of Joshua describes Joshua as an echo of Moses who engages in the same actions, only of lesser magnitude and with lesser effect. Moses leads the Israelites out of their oppression in Egypt; Joshua leads them into their domination of Canaan. Furthermore, Joshua causes the Jordan River to run dry in the same way that Moses parts the Red Sea. Finally, both Joshua and Moses perform similar administrative actions, sending out spies and allotting land to tribes. However, the differences between Moses's and Joshua's stories almost always indicate that Moses was a grander leader and prophet. While Moses communes directly with God, speaking with him face to face as though to a friend, God's presence in the Book of Joshua is largely symbolic. God exists for them in the Ark of the Covenant, a container that contains the text of Mosaic law. He does not, however, take physical form. Moses both foreshadows and overshadows Joshua.

This simplified rendering of the military campaign is contrasted by a lingering ambivalence in the behavior and the future of the Israelite people throughout Joshua. Rahab may display a blind faith in God, and the treaty with the Gibeonites may be the result of a deception, but by sparing these figures the Israelites disobey God's ongoing commandment to destroy all the native inhabitants of the promised land. Equally perplexing is the man or angel who is "the commander of the army of the Lord." He claims to be neither for nor against Israel, yet his presence at the battle of Jericho seems to connote God's blessing on Israel's military exercises. The ten chapters describing the allotment of tribal lands also undercut the decisive victories depicted in the first half of the book. Israel's resettlement is a project of enormous proportions, occurring before all the land has even been conquered. In fact, it is not clear if the remaining lands will ever be conquered; but, although God requires the total conquest of the promised land, he nevertheless gives them rest from battle (23:1). Finally, in his farewell to Israel, Joshua commands the people to throw away their religious idols and to refrain from allying with the native people. At no point do the people agree to either stipulation. Instead, they merely affirm that they will serve God (24:18, 24). Paradoxically, Joshua responds, "You cannot serve the Lord, for he is a holy God" (24:19). The ambivalence of the people regarding obedience to God in light of Joshua's persistence suggests that the future of Israel is uncertain at best.

JUDGES

SUMMARY

After Joshua's death, the tribes of Israel continue their conquest of the southern regions of Canaan, but they are unable to cleanse the land thoroughly of its native inhabitants. God declares that these remaining people will be an impediment to Israel's enjoyment of the promised land. Generations pass, and the younger Israelites turn away from God, intermarrying with the Canaanites and worshipping the local deities. God threatens to abandon Israel because of the disobedience of the youth, but he selects a series of judges, or rulers, to act as temporary leaders for the people.

Throughout the lives of these judges, the narrator tells us, Israel's behavior follows a consistent pattern: the people of Israel fall into evil, God sends a leader to save them, and, once the judge dies, the people commit even greater evil. When the Israelites' continued worship of the Canaanite gods leads to an invasion by the nation of Moab, God sends Israel a left-handed man named Ehud to be its deliverer. Ehud visits the Moabite king and offers to give the king a secret message from God. When the king dismisses his attendants, Ehud draws a sword strapped to his right thigh and plunges it into the obese king, killing him. Ehud escapes and leads the Israelites in regaining control of the Jordan River valley.

A prophet named Deborah emerges as Israel's new judge after Israel returns to evil and is invaded by a mighty army from the north. Counseling Israel's tribes under a great tree, she calls for an insurrection, and, together with God's help, the Israelites defeat the king's 900 chariots, sending the Canaanite general, Sisera, into retreat. When Sisera seeks refuge in a local woman's tent, the owner,

Jael, lures Sisera to sleep and kills him, hammering a peg into his skull. Deborah recounts the victory in a lengthy song, extolling God as a warrior and herself as the "mother in Israel" (5:7).

God commissions a humble man, Gideon, to save Israel from its next invaders, the Midianites, who impoverish and scatter the people. Gideon tears down his father's altar to the god Baal, and the Israelites respond in droves to his call to fight. God demands fewer men for the battle, and, in a test, Gideon leads the men to a river to drink. Those who cup their hands to drink are sent home, and the remaining three hundred men who lap the water with their tongues are chosen for God's army. Spying on the enemy troops at night, Gideon overhears a Midianite soldier tell his friend about a dream in which a small loaf of bread was able to knock down a large Midianite tent. The friend interprets the dream as a sign that Midian will be defeated by Israel. Gideon and his few men surround the camps, and—with the sound of trumpets and broken jars—the Israelites emit such a clamorous war cry that the Midianites turn and slay each other. Israel attempts to make Gideon its king, but Gideon refuses, proclaiming that God alone is ruler of Israel.

Widespread worship of the god Baal plagues Israel, and Gideon's son Abimelech serves a violent three-year reign as Israel's king. His tyrannical reign ends when a woman throws a millstone on Abimelech's head. Pressured by the Philistines from the east and the Ammonites from the west, Israel turns from its idol worship and God selects a new judge, Jephthah, the son of a prostitute, to challenge the Ammonites. Jephthah promises God that, if he is victorious, he will sacrifice to God the first thing that comes out of his house the day he returns from battle. Upon devastating the Ammonites, Jephthah returns home to see his daughter emerge from his house, dancing, to greet him. Jephthah laments his promise, but his daughter encourages him to remain faithful to God, and Jephthah kills the virgin girl.

The Philistines continue to oppress Israel, and the angel of God appears to a childless Israelite couple, promising them a son who will become Israel's next deliverer. The couple raises their son, Samson, as a Nazirite—a person who symbolizes his devotion to God by never cutting his hair. God blesses Samson with exceptional abilities, and one day Samson kills a lion with his bare hands. Contrary to his parents' urging, Samson chooses a Philistine woman to be his wife. During the wedding ceremony, he baffles the Philistines with a riddle, the answer to which they discover only when Samson's wife reveals the answer to them. Samson burns with anger and goes home without his wife, but when he returns to retrieve her, the Philistines have given her to another man. Samson captures three hundred foxes and ties torches to each of their tails, setting the Philistine crops ablaze. When the Philistines pursue Samson, the Israelites hand him over to his enemies, bound at the wrist. With God's power, Samson breaks his bindings and uses the jaw-bone of a donkey to kill a thousand Philistine men.

Again, Samson falls in love with a Philistine woman, Delilah. The Philistine officials urge Delilah to discover the secret of Samson's strength. Three times, Delilah asks Samson the source of his power, and Samson lies to her each time, duping the officials in their attempts to subdue him. After a while, Samson tells her the truth, informing her that his long hair is the source of his strength. While Samson is asleep, Delilah has his hair cut and alerts the officials, who capture him and gouge out his eyes. In prison, Samson's hair begins to grow again, and, during a Philistine religious festival, the blind Samson is brought out to entertain the crowds. Samson asks his servant to guide him to the pillars of the arena, and—crying out to God—Samson knocks down the pillars of the temple, killing the Philistine rulers.

Without a judge, Israel becomes even more corrupt. One day, a man and his concubine are accosted while spending the night in the Israelite tribe of Benjamin. When a gang of Benjamite men demand to have sex with the man, he offers them his concubine instead, and the men rape her repeatedly throughout the night until she dies. Enraged, the man brings the concubine home and cuts her into twelve pieces, sending a piece to each of the twelve tribes of Israel as a symbol of Israel's corruption. The rest of Israel rallies together in opposition to the tribe of Benjamin, and, with God's help, the united tribes kill more than 25,000 Benjamites. Israel grieves for its lost tribe and helps the remaining Benjamites repopulate their land.

ANALYSIS

Biblical scholars typically group the books of Joshua and Judges together, noting how well the two works complement each other. On the one hand, Joshua purports to tell a chronological history of the Hebrew conquest of Canaan, but the account and the conquest itself seem too perfect to be accurate. In contrast, Judges is a compilation of myths about the early years of the Israelite settlement. While the stories are indeed fanciful, they suggest a gradual and disjointed occupation of the promised land that is probably more true to history than the Book of Joshua. While Joshua provides a

Barnes & Noble Booksellers #2039
21001 N. Tatum Blvd. Suite 42
Phoenix, AZ 85050
480-538-8520

STR:2039 REG:002 TRN:3295 CSHR:Jenee C

Old Testament (SparkNotes Literature Gui
  9781411469655   T1
  (1 @ 5.95)   5.95

Subtotal   5.95
Sales Tax T1 (8.600%)   0.51
TOTAL   6.46
VISA   6.46
  Card#:   XXXXXXXXXXXXX3959
  Expdate: XX/XX
  Auth: 006804
  Entry Method: Chip Read

  Application Label: VISA CREDIT
  AID: a0000000031010
  TVR: 8080008000
  TSI: 6800

MEMBER WOULD HAVE SAVED   0.60

        Connect with us on Social

Facebook- @BNNorthTatum
Instagram- @bndesertridge
Twitter-   @BNDesertRidge

6.03D   05/06/2018 06:38PM

            CUSTOMER COPY

the date of return, (ii) when a gift receipt is presented within 60 days of purchase, (iii) for textbooks, (iv) when the original tender is PayPal, or (v) for products purchased at Barnes & Noble College bookstores that are listed for sale in the Barnes & Noble Booksellers inventory management system.

Opened music CDs, DVDs, vinyl records, audio books may not be returned, and can be exchanged only for the same title and only if defective. NOOKs purchased from other retailers or sellers are returnable only to the retailer or seller from which they are purchased, pursuant to such retailer's or seller's return policy. Magazines, newspapers, eBooks, digital downloads, and used books are not returnable or exchangeable. Defective NOOKs may be exchanged at the store in accordance with the applicable warranty.

Returns or exchanges will not be permitted (i) after 14 days or without receipt or (ii) for product not carried by Barnes & Noble or Barnes & Noble.com.

Policy on receipt may appear in two sections.

Return Policy

With a sales receipt or Barnes & Noble.com packing slip, a full refund in the original form of payment will be issued from any Barnes & Noble Booksellers store for returns of undamaged NOOKs, new and unread books, and unopened and undamaged music CDs, DVDs, vinyl records, toys/games and audio books made within 14 days of purchase from a Barnes & Noble Booksellers store or Barnes & Noble.com with the below exceptions:

A store credit for the purchase price will be issued (i) for purchases made by check less than 7 days prior to the date of return, (ii) when a gift receipt is presented within 60 days of purchase, (iii) for textbooks, (iv) when the original tender is PayPal, or (v) for products purchased at Barnes & Noble College bookstores that are listed for sale in the Barnes & Noble Booksellers inventory management system.

Opened music CDs, DVDs, vinyl records, audio books may not be returned, and can be exchanged only for the same title and only if defective. NOOKs purchased from other retailers or sellers are returnable only to the retailer or seller from which they are purchased, pursuant to such retailer's or seller's return policy. Magazines, newspapers, eBooks, digital downloads, and used books are not returnable or exchangeable. Defective NOOKs may be exchanged at the store in accordance with th...

methodical description of the various battles and an explanation of the distribution of land, Judges reveals the stories that the Israelite conquerors told as they gradually took over.

These individual accounts of Israel's judges are myths in the true sense of the word—not because they are false but because they are important to early Hebrew culture. The central theme of these myths is heroic struggle, chiefly of marginalized or oppressed people. The Israelites in the Book of Judges are strangers in a land they have recently conquered, and they are pressured from all sides by powerful regimes. Israel's judges manifest the virtues of this marginalized status. Jephthah is the son of a prostitute. The narrator takes pains to note that Ehud is left-handed, and it is this characteristic that enables Ehud to draw his sword and kill the Moabite king by surprise. Even more important than Deborah as a female hero is Jael, who uses the pretense of feminine warmth to draw a great commander into her tent, comforting him before she kills him.

The myth of Samson may be more appropriately described as an epic, because it is a relatively long story concerning the development of a single, extraordinary hero who, it might be said, is a metaphor for ancient Israel itself. Samson epitomizes some interesting dualities—brute nature versus civilized culture, strength versus weakness, Hebrew versus Philistine. What is unique to this story and to Judges as a whole, is that, unlike earlier books, the struggle between these opposing forces does not serve to develop irony or reversal. For Samson, the line between these distinctions is blurred. Samson—defined more by his identity as a Nazirite—is a displaced man, roaming back and forth between his home and Philistine, falling in love with Philistine women yet terrorizing the Philistines, and eventually suffering betrayal by the Israelites in return. It is only when Samson destroys the temple, crying out, "Let me die with the Philistines!" that Israel is saved through Samson's service (16:30). The epic of Samson shows that Israel's struggle—and its salvation—consists less of cleansing foreign influences from the land than of grappling with those influences while remaining faithful to God.

The stories in Judges are filled with extreme violence. This violence may cause us to question how God can be good if the greater part of the tribe of Benjamin is killed to make a religious point, or if Jephthah must keep his promise to God by killing his daughter. One answer is that the abundant violence in Israel is not due to God's wrath but to Israel's wickedness. Israel promiscuously worships other gods and insists on returning to evil despite God's help.

Another, more subtle answer, is that death in Judges is not always an absolute evil but is, at times, a thing of beauty. The tales in Judges begin to develop the notion of sacrifice—the idea that one person's death can be meaningful to another person, for religious or ethical reasons. Samson's death saves Israel from Philistine persecution, and Sisera's death at Jael's hands is a poignant symbol of Israel's victory to be celebrated in song (5:24–30). The writer tells us that the sacrifice of Jephthah's virgin daughter becomes a tradition among the Israelites, an annual celebration of the story by adolescent girls to symbolize passage from innocence into womanhood (11:39–40).

THE FIRST BOOK OF SAMUEL

> *Because you have rejected the word of the Lord, he has also rejected you from being king.*
>
> (*See* QUOTATIONS, *p. 77*)

SUMMARY

Israel's next judge, Samuel, is born to Hannah, a previously barren woman. Hannah gives Samuel to Israel's chief priest, Eli, to be raised as a Nazirite. The priesthood in Israel is in a general state of decline, and Eli's sons are disobeying God's laws. God declares that he will choose a new priest for Israel from outside Eli's family and begins delivering messages to Samuel as a young man. Samuel becomes a recognized prophet throughout Israel, delivering God's messages to the people.

During battle, the Philistines kill Eli's sons and capture the Ark of the Covenant—Israel's religious altar and symbol of God. Upon learning of the attack and robbery, Eli falls over and dies. The Ark is returned to Israel after it causes its Philistine captors to become terribly diseased. As the nation rejoices, Samuel persuades Israel to set aside its worship of local pagan deities, and God helps Israel thwart Philistine oppression for many years.

The Israelites demand that Samuel appoint a king for them so that Israel will be like other nations. Samuel is displeased, but God grants him permission to elect a king. God notes that by asking for a king, the people have not rejected Samuel; they have rejected God. Samuel warns the people that a monarchy brings certain drawbacks such as taxation, the conscription of armed forces, and the potential for tyranny, but the people are resolute.

God tells Samuel who should be king, and the following day, a man named Saul appears before Samuel, inquiring about some lost donkeys. Samuel pours oil over Saul's head to anoint him as king, and God provides a series of mystical signs to assure Saul that he should be king. Saul, who is a head taller than the average man, pleases the Israelites as king and leads them in rescuing an Israelite outpost from invasion. Stepping down as Israel's leader, Samuel encourages the people that, so long as they are obedient to God's laws, God will not punish them for requesting a king.

Despite many military victories, Saul soon disobeys God. He tries to rush into battle by performing a ritual war sacrifice without the help of a priest. Later, Samuel sends Saul to fight the Amalekites, instructing Saul to destroy them completely and leave nothing alive. Saul, however, spares the Amalekite ruler and the best portion of their flocks, hoping to present them as sacrifices to God. Samuel rebukes Saul, claiming that obedience to God's instructions is more important than religious sacrifice. He informs Saul that God will choose another man to be king of Israel. Saul pleads with Samuel, begging for forgiveness. Saul grabs for Samuel's cloak, but the cloth tears—a symbol, says Samuel, of Saul's broken kingdom.

God leads Samuel to the town of Bethlehem to choose a new king from Jesse's family. Each of Jesse's older sons are impressive, but God instructs Samuel to judge people not by their external appearances but, rather, by their hearts. Samuel anoints Jesse's youngest son, David, a shepherd, as king, and God gives divine power to David. God withdraws his power from Saul, cursing Saul with psychological distress in the form of an "evil spirit" (16:14). David begins his rise to courtly status as a harp-player for Saul during the king's emotional unrest.

The Philistines again threaten to attack Israel, this time taunting Israel with their new hero, Goliath—a giant more than nine feet tall. Saul and the Israelites tremble in fear, but David, arriving to deliver food to his brothers, offers to fight the giant. Refusing the king's armor, David publicly invokes God's help and kills Goliath with a single stone shot from his sling. The Israelites attack the retreating Philistines, and Israel returns home to the sound of women singing praises of David's victory.

Saul is insanely jealous of David, who becomes an intimate friend of Saul's son, Jonathan, and leads the Israelite troops to many more victories. After attempting to kill David with a spear, Saul sends David on a suicide mission to kill a hundred Philistine men and bring back their circumcised foreskins. David succeeds, and Saul grudgingly rewards David with his daughter Michal's hand in marriage. Saul orders his household to kill David, but, with the help of Michal and Jonathan, David flees from Saul. David builds an army of unhappy and impoverished Israelites, and he is joined by a priest who is also fleeing from Saul's destructive path.

Saul pursues David into the desert where David spares the king's life twice. While Saul is urinating in a cave, David sneaks up behind him and cuts off a corner of Saul's robe, scorning the opportunity to kill God's "annointed" ruler (24:6). At night, David and his men sneak into the king's tent and steal Saul's spear while he is sleeping. On both occasions, David announces his deed to Saul, and Saul expresses remorse both times, begging for David's mercy.

Still, Saul continues his pursuit, and David takes refuge with the Philistines, who show mercy to the great warrior and adversary of Israel's king. Preparing to fight the Philistines, Saul is wracked with fear and consults a witch, bidding the spirit medium to conjure up the dead spirit of Samuel. Samuel's ghost angrily warns Saul that he and his sons will die fighting the Philistines, ensuring the demise of Saul's kingdom. David and his men head out to fight the Amalekites, and David succeeds in destroying the warring nation. In the meantime, Saul leads Israel into a losing battle with the Philistines, and Saul's sons, including Jonathan, are killed. Saul commands his armor-bearer to kill him, but the boy refuses, and Saul falls on his own sword and dies.

ANALYSIS

The first book of Samuel tells the story of Israel's transition from a theocracy, or state ruled by a religious leader, to a monarchy, or state ruled by a political leader. Israel starts out as a nation of loosely affiliated tribes led by priests and religious heroes, but it becomes a nation-state led by a centralized king. Each stage of this transition is depicted through the narrative's three main figures: Samuel represents the old rule of the judges, Saul represents Israel's failed attempt at monarchy, and David represents God's ideal king. Although it seems logical that the rule of a single king would bring a sense of unity and cohesiveness to Israel, the opposite is the case. The move away from religious leaders divides religious and political life in Israel. Confusion about how religion and politics ought to relate to one another is the chief source of conflict in Samuel. Indeed, Saul's gravest mistake as king is his attempt to carry out the sacrificial duties of the priesthood—a role that Samuel explicitly denies the political ruler.

God's ambivalence regarding the monarchy escalates this conflict. On the one hand, God and Samuel are displeased at Israel's demand for a king, because, as God claims, this demand represents Israel's refusal to believe that God and his religious laws are adequate to rule the people. On the other hand, God willingly chooses Saul to be king, identifying Saul as the deliverer of his people. God reconciles this contradiction by distinguishing Israel's status as a human institution from its status as a divine one. As Samuel's warnings to Israel about the dangers of having a king suggest, God may bless the king, but he will not keep the king from committing the sorts of human errors and injustices that human rulers are prone to commit.

Saul's demise as king is tragic because he makes such small, human mistakes. Like all tragic heroes, Saul possesses a fatal flaw: he is more concerned with earthly objects and human customs than with spiritual or religious matters. Saul's plan to present the plunder from the Amalekites as a sacrifice to God earns Samuel's criticism because Saul mistakes a human custom for religious devotion. This criticism is symbolized by the piece of cloth that Saul is left with when he grabs at Samuel. The cloth, like all things Saul considers important, is man-made. The war song of the Israelite women, which ignites Saul's fury, further highlights Saul's flaw: "Saul has killed his thousands, / and David his ten thousands" (18:7). The refrain, which is repeated throughout the Book of Samuel by both priests and Philistines, illustrates the fact that Saul evaluates his leadership by human standards, rather than religious standards.

In contrast, God favors David because David places a higher value on religious devotion than on the physical world. David's inner virtue is Samuel's criterion for anointing him as king, and the encounter with Goliath functions as a parable for the triumph of the spiritual over the physical. The giant, a symbol of brute human force, is defeated by the diminutive David, who refuses the physical protection of the king's armor in favor of prayer, calling down God's wrath on the irreverent Goliath. David's repudiation of the physical world continues in his willingness to roam the desert on the margins of Israel, denying the opportunity to take the throne by physical force from God's current anointed ruler. Like Abraham and Moses, David reinforces God's ongoing preference for the unseen over the seen, the lesser over the greater, and inner faith over external circumstances. A commitment to these preferences seems to be the minimum religious requirement for the ideal Israelite monarch.

THE SECOND BOOK OF SAMUEL

SUMMARY

Upon learning of Saul's defeat by the Philistines, David sings a song lamenting the deaths of Saul and his friend, Jonathan. David goes to Hebron, where his followers and the southern tribe of Judah anoint him as king. Meanwhile, Saul's chief commander, Abner, garners the support of the northern tribes and instates Saul's son, Ish-Bosheth, as king of Israel. A war ensues between the conflicting regimes, played out in a series of small hand-to-hand contests between Abner's men and the army of Joab, David's general.

When Ish-Bosheth falsely accuses Abner of sleeping with one of the royal concubines, Abner defects to David's court. David welcomes Abner's support. Abner convinces the other tribes to recognize David's claim to the throne. Joab, however, seeks revenge for his brother's earlier death at Abner's hands, and he stabs Abner in secret. David's public censure of Joab and mourning for Abner wins Israel's respect, and two of Ish-Bosheth's men betray their ruler by presenting David with the severed head of the northern king. David is horrified that they have killed an innocent man, and he publicly executes these men. The united tribes declare David king of Israel.

David leads the Israelites in conquering the city of Jerusalem, a Canaanite stronghold lingering in the heart of Israel's territory. He erects his palace there and calls it "The City of David" or "Zion." Growing in power, David quells the ever-present Philistine threat in a decisive military victory. With the help of thirty thousand Israelites, David brings the Ark of the Covenant to Jerusalem in an elaborate procession. Amidst shouting and music, David dances and leaps in front of the Ark, to the embarrassment of his wife Michal. David rebukes her, claiming that he will humiliate himself as much as he wants so long as it pleases God. God is pleased that David has made a permanent home for the Ark and reveals a message to David's prophet, Nathan. God vows to grant Israel rest from foreign opposition and promises that the kingdom of David will last forever. With Joab's services, David subdues the nations of the surrounding area, expanding Israel's borders while developing diplomatic relations with the neighboring kingdoms.

One day, David watches a woman bathing from the rooftop of his palace. He summons the woman, Bathsheba, and has sex with her, and the woman becomes pregnant. Unable to disguise his indiscretion, David sends her husband, Uriah, to die on the battlefield.

SUMMARY & ANALYSIS

David marries Bathsheba, but Nathan confronts the king about his wrongdoing. Nathan tells a parable about a wealthy man who steals a poor man's only prized sheep. David is outraged by such selfishness, and Nathan informs David that the parable is about him. Nathan predicts that God will bring calamity on David's household. David repents for his wrongdoing, but, despite his fasting and praying, Bathsheba's son dies during childbirth. Afterward, David and Bathsheba have another son, Solomon.

David's older son Amnon falls in love with his half-sister Tamar and rapes her. David is furious but does nothing. Instead, Tamar's brother Absalom invites Amnon out to the country, where he and David's other sons murder Amnon. Absalom flees to a remote city for three years, but David, after mourning for Amnon, allows his son Absalom back to Jerusalem.

Absalom plots a conspiracy, forming an army and winning the hearts of the Israelite people through displays of warmth and kindness. Supported by David's chief counselor, Absalom goes to Hebron where his followers pronounce him king. Informed of this event, David flees from Jerusalem with his men, and the people of the countryside weep as he marches by. One of Saul's relatives, however, curses and throws stones at the band, gloating over David's demise. David forbids his attendants to punish the man.

Absalom enters Jerusalem where, in a display of defiance, he has sex with David's concubines. Absalom's aides advise him to attack David immediately, but one of David's officials, pretending to support Absalom, persuades Absalom to wait. This delay gives David time to muster an army, and his forces kill twenty thousand of Absalom's followers in the forests of Ephraim. Riding along, Absalom catches his head in the branches of a tree. Joab ignores David's instructions to treat Absalom gently and drives three spears into Absalom's hanging body. When David is notified of Absalom's death, he weeps, screaming repeatedly, "O my son Absalom, O Absalom, my son, my son!" (19:4).

To the frustration of his officials, David shows mercy to all of Absalom's supporters who approach him for forgiveness, especially Absalom's commander Amasa. David sends messengers to the leaders of Judah, and the tribe welcomes him back to Jerusalem. The remaining tribes—Absalom's chief supporters—fear that David will be angry at them. An uprising ensues, but Joab traps the rebels in a city and the city's residents hand over the severed head of the rebel leader. Angered that David has shown mercy to Amasa, Joab stabs Amasa one day while pretending to greet him.

David rebuilds his throne with continued acts of local diplomacy and with military victories over the Philistines. He composes a song praising God as a loving and kind deliverer, and the narrator briefly recounts the feats of David's most famous fighting men.

ANALYSIS

The major scholarly debate over 2 Samuel involves whether or not the book describes David in a negative or positive light. Chapters 9–20 of 2 Samuel are not necessarily complimentary. David commits adultery, tries to have his mistress's husband killed, and loses control of his sons. At the same time, however, the narrator explains how each of these incidents actually proves David's righteousness. Not only are David's sons blamed for their own actions, but David's own repentance for his misdeeds is described as exemplary. The circumstances surrounding David's reign suggest that God approves of David's actions. David's kingdom in Zion represents the fulfillment of God's promises to Abraham, Jacob, and Moses. It establishes the unified tribes of Israel in the promised land under the rule of a divinely sanctioned leader. David's triumphal entry into Jerusalem with the Ark of the Covenant marks the story's climax, symbolizing the ideal combination of religion and politics in Israel and the peaceful unification of God and man in one city. The image of an organized procession of song and dance around a symbol of God suggests that the people have, temporarily, reconciled their earthly aspirations with their religious commitments. 2 Samuel is characterized by the contrast between joyful images and images of civil conflict and confusion. All of the challengers to David's throne in Samuel lose their heads, symbolizing their thwarted attempts to become the head of Israel. David's retreat from Jerusalem to the sound of weeping and cursing contrasts with his earlier celebratory march into the city. Geographical motifs further reinforce this sense of division and loss. Ish-Bosheth's challenge to the throne divides Israel into two halves, northern and southern. Absalom is declared king outside of Jerusalem in Hebron, a symbol of his dissent from David, while his exhibition at the top of the palace represents his ascent to power. David, meanwhile, must move out from the center of Israel and across the Jordan River—the chief mark of one's exile from the promised land.

SUMMARY & ANALYSIS

Individual characters express differing opinions about David's method of ruling. In one sense, David's mercy shows great prudence, for his tolerance of Ish-Bosheth eventually earns the respect of Ish-Bosheth's subjects. However, David's reluctance to punish Amnon for the rape of Tamar seems more permissive than just, and only fosters Absalom's rage. Joab similarly believes that David's kindness to Abner and Amasa is the result of oversight. Joab's decision to take matters into his own hands makes Joab a foil to David. While Joab is suspicious of others and concerned with end results, David is trusting and believes that an earnest response in the present moment is more important than outcomes. David's trust in the impulses of the present moment is the source of his greatest failing, his lust for Bathsheba. David's immediate impulses are also the source of the narrative's greatest moment of pathos—David's desperate cries for Absalom. Nevertheless, his mercy stabilizes Israel by providing second chances, not only to political rebels, but to some of the nation's most intriguing characters, such as Saul's cursing relative.

THE FIRST & SECOND BOOKS OF KINGS

SUMMARY

David is old and bed-ridden, and his son Adonijah proclaims himself king with the help of David's commander Joab and the priest, Abiathar. Hearing this news, David instructs the prophet Nathan to anoint David's son, Solomon, as king. The people rally behind Solomon in a grand procession to the royal throne. Before dying, David charges Solomon to remain faithful to God and his laws. Solomon solidifies his claim to the throne by killing Joab, Adonijah, and the remaining dissenters from David's reign. He also makes an alliance with Egypt by marrying the pharaoh's daughter.

Because Solomon carefully obeys God's laws, God appears to him in a dream and offers to grant the new king one wish. Solomon asks for wisdom to govern with justice and to know the difference between right and wrong. God is so impressed with Solomon's humble request that he promises Solomon the additional gifts of wealth and long life. As a result, Solomon lives in great opulence and his empire stretches from Egypt to the Euphrates River. He earns international fame for his wise sayings and scientific knowledge.

With his vast resources, Solomon builds an elaborate temple to God as well as a palace for himself in Jerusalem. Construction begins exactly four hundred and eighty years after Israel's exodus from Egypt. Solomon conscripts thousands of laborers for the work and imports materials from neighboring countries. The Temple is lined with gold and features large, hand-sculpted angels and pillars. Solomon places the Ark of the Covenant inside, and all of Israel gathers for the dedication. After sacrificing herds of animals on the altar, Solomon prays for God's blessing on the Temple. God appears to Solomon and promises to dwell in the Temple so long as Solomon and the Israelites are obedient to his laws. If they are not, God will remove his presence from the Temple, destroying both the temple and the nation.

Solomon's success continues until he marries many foreign women. They influence him to worship and erect altars to foreign deities. God is infuriated and tells Solomon that he will dismember the kingdom. God will tear away all of the tribes from Solomon's kingdom except for one, Judah. God allows the tribe of Judah to remain since Solomon is David's son. Following God's declaration, a prophet meets one of Solomon's officials, Jeroboam, with a cloak torn into twelve pieces, representing the twelve tribes of Israel. The prophet hands Jeroboam ten of the twelve pieces and explains that God has chosen him to rule these selected tribes as Israel's new king.

Solomon dies, and his son Rehoboam assumes the throne. Led by Jeroboam, the people gather before the young king to request that Rehoboam treat them more kindly than Solomon did during his reign. Rehoboam is headstrong and refuses, threatening to punish and enslave the people. The Israelites unite in rebellion, cursing the tribe of Judah and eluding Rehoboam's attempts to forcefully subdue them. They head north, where they crown Jeroboam king of Israel in the city of Shechem. Israel splits into two kingdoms: the kingdom of Israel in the north, and the kingdom of Judah in the south.

To distinguish the new, separate kingdom of Israel from the old kingdom in Jerusalem, Jeroboam erects altars and shrines to golden calves throughout the northern land. The Israelites worship the idols, and the Levite priests, formerly devoted to God, serve them as well. One day, Jeroboam's son is ill, and his wife approaches a prophet to seek guidance. The prophet warns that Jeroboam's household will be destroyed and that Israel will eventually lose control of the promised land because of Jeroboam's abhorrent practices. One generation later, Jeroboam's entire family is slaughtered when another Israelite takes the throne by force.

Meanwhile, King Rehoboam also erects altars and shrines to idols in Judah, even authorizing male and female prostitution in

SUMMARY & ANALYSIS

these shrines. The two kingdoms, northern and southern, continue to fight each other. After Rehoboam and Jeroboam die, the narrator recounts the story of all the succeeding kings in each kingdom, summarizing each king's reign by whether he does good or evil. Almost all of Israel's northern kings commit great evil, expanding on the practices of their fathers. Some of the southern kings in Jerusalem try to revive obedience to God, but none of them bans the worship of foreign gods in Judah.

With the help of his wife Jezebel, Ahab, northern Israel's most wicked king, spreads cult worship of the god Baal throughout the northern lands. In response, a prophet named Elijah emerges and informs Ahab that God will curse the land with a great drought. Elijah leads a secluded life on the outskirts of civilization. Ravens bring Elijah food and he performs miracles for the local people. After three years of drought, Queen Jezebel begins a campaign to murder all of God's prophets in the land. Elijah publicly confronts Ahab, demanding that the Israelite people profess allegiance to either God or Baal. The people do not respond. Elijah challenges the priests of Baal to a contest to see whose god can miraculously set an unlit animal sacrifice on fire. Despite animated prayer and self-mutilation, the priests of Baal are unable to ignite their altar. Elijah soaks his altar in water three times, and, when he prays, God engulfs the altar in flames.

Elijah flees from the belligerent Jezebel into the desert. He complains to God that, despite his earnest service, the Israelites continue to be disobedient. God promises to show himself to Elijah. Elijah is surrounded by wind, earthquakes, and fire, but none of these, we are told, is God. Instead, Elijah hears a soft whisper amidst the storm, and he recognizes that this is God. Encouraged, Elijah returns to civilization where he appoints a new man, Elisha, to be his apprentice and to eventually succeed him as prophet.

One day, Ahab and Jezebel steal a man's vineyard by slandering the man's name in public until the citizens stone the man. Elijah finds Ahab in the vineyard and declares that because of their murderous deeds, Ahab and Jezebel will die and dogs will lick up their blood. Soon after, King Ahab makes a rare pact with the king of Judah. The two lead their united forces against the Arameans who are occupying Israel's borders. Ahab is killed and bleeds to death in his chariot. When the chariot is cleaned after battle, dogs gather to lick his blood.

Not long after, Elijah is miraculously taken up into heaven by a flaming chariot, never to return, while Elisha looks on. Elisha assumes Elijah's role as prophet, acting as a cryptic doomsayer to Israel's kings while performing miracles for the common folk. Elisha helps a barren woman become pregnant, and when her young son suddenly dies, Elisha brings the boy back to life by lying on top of him. He guides the king of Israel in eluding the Aramean invaders from the north by plaguing the enemy troops with blindness.

Elisha initiates a coup to cut off Ahab and Jezebel's dynasty by secretly anointing a military commander, Jehu, to overthrow the throne. Jehu descends on the city where the current king, who is Ahab's son, and Judah's king are visiting each other. The men of the city rapidly defect to Jehu's side. Jehu overcomes the kings on horseback and shoots them with an arrow, decrying their witchcraft and idolatry in the process. Entering the city, Jezebel calls out seductively to Jehu from a window. The men of the city throw her out the window, and Jehu's horses trample her. The dogs eat her dead body, fulfilling Elijah's prophecy. After killing the rest of Ahab's family, Jehu invites all the priests of Baal to an assembly and murders them. He wipes out the Baal cult in Israel, but he does not forbid the worship of other gods.

The narrator continues the chronological account of Israel and Judah's kings. Each of Israel's kings is more evil than the previous, and Northern Israel gradually loses its territories to Assyrian pressure from the northeast. Assyria finally invades the northern kingdom of Israel entirely and captures the Israelites, removing them to Assyria. God's presence leaves the people of Israel, and scattered Near-Eastern groups populate the promised land, worshipping their own gods.

A handful of Judah's kings make a brave attempt at reform in the southern kingdom. Two kings embark on repairing the decaying Temple in Jerusalem. When Hezekiah assumes the throne, he destroys all of the altars and idols in Judah—the first such policy since Rehoboam introduced the idols into the land. With the help of the great prophet Isaiah, Judah thwarts heavy economic and military threats from Assyria. Finally, Judah's king Josiah directs a national program of spiritual renewal. He reads the Laws of Moses in front of all the people, and the people reaffirm their commitment to God's covenant, celebrating the Passover for the first time in centuries. Despite these attempts to turn the religious tide in Judah, however, evil rulers regain power after Josiah's death. The king of Babylon invades the southern kingdom of Israel, burning Jerusalem and destroying the Temple. Like their northern brothers, the people of Judah are exiled, settling in Babylon far away from their homeland.

ANALYSIS

The two volumes of Kings continue the story of Israel's tumultuous monarchy begun in Genesis and continued in the books of Samuel. The history spans almost four hundred years of events in ancient Israel. From the beginning of Solomon's reign in around 965 B.C. to the fall of the northern and southern kingdoms in 722 B.C. and 567 B.C., respectively, the nation of Israel dominates the international affairs of the Near East. As a result, many of the events described in the biblical account of Israel's divided kingdom can be authenticated historically. However, the authors of Kings do not simply list Israel and Judah's kings, but arrange their stories in a way that highlights the direct connection between Israel's religious infidelity and its radical political demise.

Solomon's temple is a monolithic symbol that changes to reflect the changing fortunes of the Israelites. The author interprets the temple's construction as a sign that Israel, the land originally promised to Moses, has arrived. By noting that Solomon builds it in "the four hundred and eightieth year after the Israelites came out of the land of Egypt," the narrator suggests that all of Israel's struggles to enter and conquer the promised land have prepared this moment (6:1). The Temple's large, solid structure is a physical manifestation of Israel's secure position in the land. God proves a spiritual manifestation of Israel's security when he promises to reside in the temple, placing his "name there forever" (9:3). The fact that the Temple is a man-made object that can decay foreshadows the eventual spiritual decay of Israel. Furthermore, the importance of a physical object to Solomon and the people contrasts with the importance in earlier biblical books of incorporeal spiritual elements. The temple also reflects the downfall of Israel. After the author spends four chapters detailing its construction and dedication, the Temple disappears from the narrative just as Israel's religious commitment to God fades from the minds of its rulers. Its final destruction at the hands of the Babylonians mirrors Israel's total neglect of God's covenant.

Part of the purpose of the books of Kings is to provide a cultural history of Israel that the Israelites can read to understand the history of their people. The authors and compilers of the books use rhetorical devices to reflect this purpose. One such device is the simultaneous telling of the histories of Israel and Judah. Accounts of Israelite kings always accompany accounts of contemporary kings in Judah. The narrator then describes how God views each king. This rhetorical device labels each king's reign as good or evil, and provides a moral evaluation of Israel and Judah's history. Judah appears generally more good than Israel since it has more good kings, a trend that reflects God's promise to Solomon that he will bless Judah because it is the site of King David's legacy in Jerusalem. On the whole, however, both Judah and Israel have a majority of evil kings. In spite of Hezekiah and Josiah's laudable reforms in Judah, the attacks by Assyria and Babylon appear to be punishment for the religious deterioration of the Israelites.

As the books' religious protagonists, Elijah and Elisha illustrate that the nature of prophets has changed throughout the Old Testament. Moses, Joshua, the judges, and David are all leaders of the Israelites, and, as the people's representatives, they meet with God on mountains or in religious centers to intercede on behalf of the people for their wrongdoing. Elijah and Elisha, however, are located on the outskirts of communities, and they utter mystical warnings or oracles to Israel that are fatalistic at best. Rather than leading the people to greatness, Elijah's contest with the priests of Baal is merely an attempt to diminish the people's ongoing evil, and Elisha's healing of the peasant boy only helps to ease pain. The narrator mentions Elisha's death only in passing, and Elijah is not actually buried in Israel. He is, instead, taken straight into heaven by supernatural means, an event that suggests that the land is too evil for God's prophets. Whereas God formerly presents himself to Moses using thunder and lightning, God's small, gentle whisper to Elijah shows that the people's worship of other deities has effectively quelled God's voice in Israel.

JOB

If I sin, what do I do to you, you watcher of humanity?
Why have you made me your target?

(See QUOTATIONS, *p. 78)*

SUMMARY
Job is a wealthy man living in a land called Uz with his large family and extensive flocks. He is "blameless" and "upright," always careful to avoid doing evil (1:1). One day, Satan ("the Adversary") appears before God in heaven. God boasts to Satan about Job's

goodness, but Satan argues that Job is only good because God has blessed him abundantly. Satan challenges God that, if given permission to punish the man, Job will turn and curse God. God allows Satan to torment Job to test this bold claim, but he forbids Satan to take Job's life in the process.

In the course of one day, Job receives four messages, each bearing separate news that his livestock, servants, and ten children have all died due to marauding invaders or natural catastrophes. Job tears his clothes and shaves his head in mourning, but he still blesses God in his prayers. Satan appears in heaven again, and God grants him another chance to test Job. This time, Job is afflicted with horrible skin sores. His wife encourages him to curse God and to give up and die, but Job refuses, struggling to accept his circumstances.

Three of Job's friends, Eliphaz, Bildad, and Zophar, come to visit him, sitting with Job in silence for seven days out of respect for his mourning. On the seventh day, Job speaks, beginning a conversation in which each of the four men shares his thoughts on Job's afflictions in long, poetic statements.

Job curses the day he was born, comparing life and death to light and darkness. He wishes that his birth had been shrouded in darkness and longs to have never been born, feeling that light, or life, only intensifies his misery. Eliphaz responds that Job, who has comforted other people, now shows that he never really understood their pain. Eliphaz believes that Job's agony must be due to some sin Job has committed, and he urges Job to seek God's favor. Bildad and Zophar agree that Job must have committed evil to offend God's justice and argue that he should strive to exhibit more blameless behavior. Bildad surmises that Job's children brought their deaths upon themselves. Even worse, Zophar implies that whatever wrong Job has done probably deserves greater punishment than what he has received.

Job responds to each of these remarks, growing so irritated that he calls his friends "worthless physicians" who "whitewash [their advice] with lies" (13:4). After making pains to assert his blameless character, Job ponders man's relationship to God. He wonders why God judges people by their actions if God can just as easily alter or forgive their behavior. It is also unclear to Job how a human can appease or court God's justice. God is unseen, and his ways are inscrutable and beyond human understanding. Moreover, humans cannot possibly persuade God with their words. God cannot be deceived, and Job admits that he does not even understand himself well enough to effectively plead his case to God. Job wishes for someone who can mediate between himself and God, or for God to send him to Sheol, the deep place of the dead.

Job's friends are offended that he scorns their wisdom. They think his questions are crafty and lack an appropriate fear of God, and they use many analogies and metaphors to stress their ongoing point that nothing good comes of wickedness. Job sustains his confidence in spite of these criticisms, responding that even if he has done evil, it is his own personal problem. Furthermore, he believes that there is a "witness" or a "Redeemer" in heaven who will vouch for his innocence (16:19, 19:25). After a while, the upbraiding proves too much for Job, and he grows sarcastic, impatient, and afraid. He laments the injustice that God lets wicked people prosper while he and countless other innocent people suffer. Job wants to confront God and complain, but he cannot physically find God to do it. He feels that wisdom is hidden from human minds, but he resolves to persist in pursuing wisdom by fearing God and avoiding evil.

Without provocation, another friend, Elihu, suddenly enters the conversation. The young Elihu believes that Job has spent too much energy vindicating himself rather than God. Elihu explains to Job that God communicates with humans by two ways—visions and physical pain. He says that physical suffering provides the sufferer with an opportunity to realize God's love and forgiveness when he is well again, understanding that God has "ransomed" him from an impending death (33:24). Elihu also assumes that Job must be wicked to be suffering as he is, and he thinks that Job's excessive talking is an act of rebellion against God.

God finally interrupts, calling from a whirlwind and demanding Job to be brave and respond to his questions. God's questions are rhetorical, intending to show how little Job knows about creation and how much power God alone has. God describes many detailed aspects of his creation, praising especially his creation of two large beasts, the Behemoth and Leviathan. Overwhelmed by the encounter, Job acknowledges God's unlimited power and admits the limitations of his human knowledge. This response pleases God, but he is upset with Eliphaz, Bildad, and Zophar for spouting poor and theologically unsound advice. Job intercedes on their behalf, and God forgives them. God returns Job's health, providing him with twice as much property as before, new children, and an extremely long life.

ANALYSIS

The Book of Job is one of the most celebrated pieces of biblical literature, not only because it explores some of the most profound questions humans ask about their lives, but also because it is extremely well written. The work combines two literary forms, framing forty chapters of verse between two and a half chapters of prose at the beginning and the end. The poetic discourse of Job and his friends is unique in its own right. The lengthy conversation has the unified voice and consistent style of poetry, but it is a dialogue between characters who alter their moods, question their motives, change their minds, and undercut each other with sarcasm and innuendo. Although Job comes closest to doing so, no single character articulates one true or authoritative opinion. Each speaker has his own flaws as well as his own lofty moments of observation or astute theological insight.

The interaction between Job and his friends illustrates the painful irony of his situation. Our knowledge that Job's punishment is the result of a contest between God and Satan contrasts with Job's confusion and his friends' lecturing, as they try to understand why Job is being punished. The premise of the friends' argument is that misfortune only follows from evil deeds. Bildad instructs Job, "if you are pure and upright, / surely then [God] will rouse himself / for you" and he later goads Job to be a "blameless person" (8:6, 8:20). The language in these passages is ironic, since, unbeknownst to Job or Job's friends, God and Satan do in fact view Job as "blameless and upright." This contrast shows the folly of the three friends who ignore Job's pain while purporting to encourage him. The interaction also shows the folly of trying to understand God's ways. The three friends and Job have a serious theological conversation about a situation that actually is simply a game between God and Satan. The fault of Job and his friends lies in trying to explain the nature of God with only the limited information available to human knowledge, as God himself notes when he roars from the whirlwind, "Who is this that darkness counsel / by words without / knowledge?" (38:2).

The dominant theme of Job is the difficulty of understanding why an all-powerful God allows good people to suffer. Job wants to find a way to justify God's actions, but he cannot understand why there are evil people who "harm the childless woman, / and do no good to the widow," only to be rewarded with long, successful lives (24:21). Job's friends, including Elihu, say that God distributes

SUMMARY & ANALYSIS

outcomes to each person as his or her actions deserve. As a result of this belief, they insist that Job has committed some wrongdoing to merit his punishment. God himself declines to present a rational explanation for the unfair distribution of blessings among men. He boasts to Job, "Have you comprehended the / expanse of the earth? / Declare, if you know all this" (38:18). God suggests that people should not discuss divine justice since God's power is so great that humans cannot possibly justify his ways.

One of the chief virtues of the poetry in Job is its rhetoric. The book's rhetorical language seeks to produce an effect in the listener rather than communicate a literal idea. God's onslaught of rhetorical questions to Job, asking if Job can perform the same things he can do, overwhelms both Job and the reader with the sense of God's extensive power as well as his pride. Sarcasm is also a frequent rhetorical tool for Job and his friends in their conversation. After Bildad lectures Job about human wisdom, Job sneers, "How you have helped one / who has no power! / How you have assisted the arm / that has no strength!" (26:2). Job is saying that he already knows what Bildad has just explained about wisdom. The self-deprecating tone and sarcastic response are rare elements in ancient verse. Such irony not only heightens the playfulness of the text but suggests the characters are actively responding to each other, thus connecting their seemingly disparate speeches together. The poetry in Job is a true dialogue, for the characters develop ideas and unique personalities throughout the course of their responses.

ECCLESIASTES

> For everything there is a season, and a time for every matter under heaven: a time to be born, and a time to die.... *(See* QUOTATIONS, *p. 79)*

SUMMARY

The narrator of Ecclesiastes is a nameless person who calls himself a "Teacher," and identifies himself as the current king of Israel and a son of King David. The Teacher opens with the exclamation, "Vanity of vanities . . . ! All is vanity" (1:2). He laments that everything in life is endless and meaningless—especially human toil and the cycles of nature—for nothing is ever truly new on earth. As the wisest man in Jerusalem, the Teacher feels he is cursed with the unhappy task of discerning wisdom, for he has seen "all the deeds that are done under the sun" (1:14). In a mixture of prose and verse, the Teacher compiles his studies, hypotheses, and proverbs regarding wisdom.

The Teacher tries many earthly pleasures. He drinks, becomes wealthy, acquires power, buys property, experiences sexual gratification, and views artistic entertainment. However, none of these experiences satisfies him. Although the Teacher originally assumes that wisdom is better than folly, he realizes that achieving wisdom is a frustrating and elusive pursuit, for the wise and the foolish both die the same death. He hypothesizes that the best humans can do is to honor God and to eat, drink, and enjoy themselves.

The Teacher also surveys the general trends of human activity. He notes that just as there is time for each good thing in life, such as birth or love, there is always a time for its opposite, such as death or hate. It is often hard for mortal humans to understand the difference between wickedness and justice, but God distinguishes between the two. The Teacher notes that human labor is marked by competition, envy, and oppression. The Teacher praises the virtues of human cooperation, noting the advantages that a team of two or three individuals has over one person alone.

Next, the Teacher discusses various foolish actions, such as gluttony, the love of money, and excessive talking. The Teacher provides a series of instructions for avoiding such foolhardiness. Each saying extols negative experiences over positive ones: mourning, he claims, is better than feasting, and the end of things is better than the beginning. He also encourages people to be neither too righteous nor too wicked but to remain moderate.

Still, the Teacher remains bothered by the fact that both evil and good people meet the same fate. He grows tired of discussing the distinctions between good and bad, clean and unclean, obedient and disobedient. He ultimately decides that the only factors in determining the outcome between life's opposing forces are time and chance.

The Teacher gives positive exhortations. He encourages humans to enjoy their vain lives and activities to the fullest. People must embrace the unforeseen chances of life, since caution only impedes God's providence. He urges young people to remain happy and to follow their inclinations, reminding them to always remember God. The things of earth are only temporary, and life is a cycle that eventually returns to God (12:7). The Teacher also warns the reader against heeding too many wise sayings, for the study of wisdom never ends. The "end of the matter," he concludes, is for humans to fear God and to obey his commandments (12:13).

ANALYSIS

The Book of Ecclesiastes is a notoriously confusing portion of the Old Testament. The Teacher is uncertain and ambiguous in his writing. His claims suggest that the Teacher is the great King Solomon—the son of King David whom God blesses with powers of immense wisdom. While this identity lends credibility to the book, the Teacher's comments are not at all systematic. The book is often repetitive or contradictory. The frequent changes in tone make it unclear whether the Teacher intends his comments to describe how humans naturally behave or to tell people how they should behave. The Teacher's recurring lament of "vanity" is emblematic of the book's elusive intentions. "Vanity" is a translation of the Hebrew word *hebel,* which means "breath of the wind," connoting uselessness, deceptiveness, and transience. Indeed, the Teacher's confusing style may be a means to reinforce his argument that human wisdom is essentially limited or "vain."

Ecclesiastes' manner of teaching contrasts with the rest of the Old Testament because it questions the process of receiving wisdom and ideals. Although much of the Old Testament is aimed at setting up absolute opposites, The Teacher is skeptical of such binary opposites. He does not endorse the division of the world into positive and negative forces, including good and evil, peace and war, clean and unclean. The Teacher does not believe that these forces do not exist, but he suggests that defining life within such simplistic terms may not be an effective way for human beings to understand it. In his most famous verse, he notes that each experience has its appropriate place in life: there is "a time to keep silence, and a time / to speak; / a time to love, and a time to hate . . ." (3:7–8). This verse suggests that the tension between positive and negative experiences is fundamental to human life, and that only God can truly judge when a situation is either good or evil. Later, he assumes a more pessimistic tone, affirming that time and chance are the only determining factors in the race between good and evil. The premise of this point of view is that the difference between good and evil is so subtle and transient that humans cannot confidently assume they are able to differentiate between good and evil or between obedience and disobedience.

The Teacher's mode of argument is consistent with his beliefs about the limitations of human reason. Rather than providing us with a set of general rules or guidelines for wise behavior, the Teacher makes a series of observations about concrete human experiences. The Teacher's study of human pleasure is empirical, testing each pleasurable experience and forming conclusions only on the basis of observations. The Teacher also refers to what he sees or finds in life rather than what he thinks. He says, "See, this is what I found . . . adding one thing to another to find the sum, which my mind has sought repeatedly, but I have not found" (7:27). The "sum," or final meaning, of human life eludes the Teacher, and he prefers to base his thoughts on his experiences. The Teacher's proverbs and sayings focus on concrete objects and feelings. To encourage humans to embrace life's chances, he instructs, "Send out your bread upon the waters . . ." (11:1). He also speaks about walking on the road, charming snakes, digging pits, looking at the sun, and, as always, his chief advice is to eat, drink, and be merry. These sayings are metaphors and symbols for diverse experiences from which larger conclusions can be drawn; but the Teacher leaves the interpretation of his sayings to the reader, further emphasizing his distaste for rigid or dogmatic wisdom.

PSALMS

OVERVIEW

A psalm is a religious poem or song set to music. Some of the psalms in the Book of Psalms are hymns to be sung by a congregation, and "Songs of Ascent" to be sung by pilgrims approaching the Temple. Some are private prayers, and some are lyrical devices for recalling historical events in Israel's history. In its current form, the Book of Psalms contains one hundred and fifty individual psalms, although this number may vary in different biblical translations.

Traditionally, the psalms are separated into five books, and many poems are further distinguished by brief titles attributing the given work to a specific author, though these titles were probably added at a later date by an editor or group of editors of the psalms; the authorship of the psalms is uncertain at best. Because the subject matter of the psalms ranges from the events of King David's dynasty to the exile of the Israelites in Babylon, the poems may have been composed anywhere from the tenth century B.C. to the sixth century B.C. or later.

Many of the psalms rehearse episodes of Israel's history, especially the story of Israel's exodus from Egypt and its arrival in the promised land. Psalm 137 is a beautiful lament of the early days of

Israel's captivity in Babylon. The poem opens with the image of the Israelites weeping by the banks of the Babylonian rivers, longing for Jerusalem, or Zion. When their captors ask the Israelites to sing for them, the Israelites refuse, hanging their harps on the branches of the willow trees. The poet asks, "How could we sing the Lord's / song / in a foreign land?" (137:4). The poem ends with a call for vengeance on the Babylonians. It acts as an earnest reminder both to the exiled Israelites and to later biblical readers of the importance of the promised land for the celebration of the Jewish faith.

TYPES OF PSALMS

A majority of the biblical psalms are devoted to expressing praise or thanksgiving to God. Psalm 8, for instance, is a communal or public declaration of praise to God for his relationship with creation. The poet praises God for his command over each level of creation, beginning with the cosmos, then descending gradually to humankind, the animals, and, lastly, the sea. The speaker expresses amazement that God, who is above the heavens, not only concerns himself with the welfare of humans but places humans directly beneath himself in importance, granting them authority over the rest of creation, which is "under their feet" (8:6). Poems such as Psalm 46 praise "the city of God" or "Zion" for being God's home, and many of the psalms suggest a grand entrance to Jerusalem, such as Psalm 100: "Enter his gates with thanksgiving, / and his courts with praise" (100:4). Similarly, when the speaker says in Psalm 121, "I lift my eyes to the hills," the poem conveys the expectation and longing of the Jewish worshipper as he approaches the Temple in Jerusalem (121:1).

Another category of psalms includes laments or supplications, poems in which the author requests relief from his physical suffering and his enemies. These enemies may be actual, such as opposing nations or public accusers, or they may be figurative depictions of an encroaching spiritual evil. In Psalm 22, the speaker characterizes the band of nondescript evildoers that trouble the poet as a series of approaching ravenous animals—first bulls, then roaring lions, and then dogs. The evildoers surround the speaker, staring at and gloating over his now shriveled and emaciated body, finally stripping him of his clothes. In verse nineteen, the speaker cries for God's relief, and God proceeds to deliver him from each of the three beasts in reverse order—first from the dog, then from the lion, and finally from the wild oxen. God's sudden rescue complete, the psalm of lament becomes a psalm of thanksgiving as the speaker vows to announce God's praises to all of Israel.

Supplication and lament are integral parts of another type of psalm, in which the poet moves from despair over his own wrong-doing to a profession of deeper faith in God. These are some of the most beloved psalms, for they are deeply personal poems that offer hope of redemption for the individual. The poet decries his spiritual despair using metaphors similar to the psalms of lament. In Psalm 40, the poet is stuck in a "desolate / pit" and a "miry bog" until God sets him "upon a rock" (40:2). The poet walks through dark valleys in Psalm 23, his body wastes away in Psalm 32, and his bones are crushed in Psalm 51. God relieves the poet by acting as a "refuge," a "strong fortress," and a "hiding place" (31:2, 32:7).

Psalms devoted to wisdom use proverbs or catchy rhetorical de-vices to give moral instructions to the reader. For example, Psalm 127 opens with a quaint proverb to encourage the listener's devo-tion to God: "Unless the Lord builds the house, / those who build it labor in vain" (127:1). Psalm 119, the longest psalm in the Bible with 176 verses, is a meditation on God's law using an *acrostic*—a poem in which each segment begins with a consecutive letter of the Hebrew alphabet.

Poetic Form and Style

The poet of Psalms consistently uses parallelism to enhance his meaning. Unlike Roman poetry, in which rhythm and meter are structured around a pattern of stressed syllables, biblical poetry is largely based on pairings of "versets"—segments or halves of verses and lines, usually only a handful of words long. These versets "par-allel" each other, the second verset reiterating or expanding upon the ideas of the first verset. Sometimes, parallel versets repeat the same words:

> *The voice of the Lord breaks the cedars;*
> *the Lord breaks the cedars of Lebanon.*   *(29:5)*

More often, however, parallel versets repeat meaning. In Psalm 40:8, the speaker says,

> *I delight to do your will, O my God;*
> *your law is within my heart.*   *(40:8)*

Here, the poet restates that obedience to God is very important to him. The second line, however, offers the reader new and more specific information, affirming, in figurative language, that God's commandments are so precious to the speaker that they reside in his heart. In this way, the parallelism of meaning in biblical poetry is not just a system of redundant lines. Rather, parallelism of meaning helps develop the imagery and ideas within each psalm by creating the occasion for analogies, greater detail, and showing how one event or idea follows from another.

Despite the sheer number and variety of the psalms, the metaphors throughout the one hundred and fifty poems are consistent. The poet's enemies are typically described as listless or transient creatures, usually wild animals or approaching natural catastrophes. Psalm 91 characterizes the speaker's enemies as "deadly pestilence," as well as lions and serpents, and Psalm 1 compares the wicked to chaff blowing in the wind. The poet or protagonist, on the other hand, is typically one who is lost or displaced. In Psalm 42, the poet refers to himself as a deer searching for flowing streams, and in other poems, the speaker is wandering on a dangerous path or stuck in a ditch or a bog. God, however, is frequently spoken of in geological or geographical terms. He is a rock, a refuge, and a fortress; he resides in the hills and, more importantly, in Zion, the city of Jerusalem. In a sense, God is himself a location, a "hiding place" in Psalm 32 and someone who draws "boundary lines" for the poet (16:6). Even as a shepherd in Psalm 23, God directs the wandering poet to "green pastures" and welcomes him to a table—a centralized location. These images of God as a place of protection that is somehow united with the land elaborate the promised land of the Old Testament as a symbol of Israel's religious well-being.

THE SONG OF SOLOMON

SUMMARY
The Song of Solomon is a series of lyrical poems organized as a lengthy dialogue between a young woman and her lover. A third party, or chorus, occasionally addresses the lovers. The first poem is spoken by the young maiden, who longs to be near her lover and enjoy his kisses. She explains that she has a dark complexion because her family sends her to work in the vineyards. She searches for her lover, comparing him to a wandering shepherd, and the chorus encourages her to follow the flocks to his tent.

The lovers lie on a couch together. The man praises the beauty of his beloved, comparing her to a young mare and comparing her eyes to doves' eyes. He describes verdant and fertile surroundings. The maiden calls herself a rose and a lily, covered by the shade of her beloved, a fruit tree. She compares her beloved to a lively gazelle that arrives to take her away during spring when the plants are budding. The maiden boasts that the man now pastures his flocks of sheep among her lilies. She warns other women, "the daughters of Jerusalem," not to fall in love too early (2:7).

While in bed, the maiden dreams that she is searching the city streets for her lover and that she finds him and takes him home. She envisions a lavish wedding procession, in which her happy bridegroom appears as King Solomon. The man speaks, comparing each part of the maiden's body to animals and precious objects. He calls for her to come down from the mountain peaks to be with him. With intense yearning, he characterizes her as an enclosed "garden" full of ripe foliage and a flowing fountain (4:12–15). The maiden bids the wind to blow on her garden and invites the man into the garden. The man dines in the garden and calls for their friends to celebrate with the lovers.

In another dream, the maiden hears her lover knocking at her door late one night, but he disappears. Again, she roams the streets, but this time the city guards accost the maiden. She asks the "daughters of Jerusalem" to help her find her lover. The chorus asks her to describe the young man, and she compares each part of his body to precious metals, jewels, and animals.

The two find each other in the garden. The man continues to praise each part of the maiden's body. He bids her to dance and likens her to a palm tree with breasts like fruit. The maiden invites her lover to the fields and villages, promising to give him her love among the blossoming vineyards. She wishes that he were her brother so that people would not comment about their open displays of affection. She urges him to "seal" his heart with her love, for love is strong. The maiden thinks back on her earlier chastity but is glad she has lost it peacefully "in his eyes" (8:10). The man says that, while King Solomon may have many vineyards, he is happy with his one vineyard, the maiden.

ANALYSIS

The Song of Solomon is also called "The Song of Songs," suggesting that it is the greatest of all songs. The first title implies that King Solomon composed the collection of love poems, but Solomon's name was probably added at a later date by the song's editors, perhaps because of references within the text to the wise and prolific king. This attribution to Solomon led to the book's inclusion in the Hebrew Bible and later, Christian versions of the Old Testament. Early Hebrew and Christian scholars long maintained that the love story is an allegory of God's love for humankind, or of the intensity of divine love within the human heart. However, it is undeniable that the song celebrates not only human love but also the sensuous and mystical quality of erotic desire.

Modern scholars see similarities between The Song of Solomon and other ancient Near-Eastern stories in which the fertility of the earth depends upon the sexual encounter of a male and female deity. Although the biblical maiden and her lover themselves do not affect the fertility of the land, there are numerous parallels between the fertile vegetation of their surroundings and the success of their romance. The lovers recline on a green couch, whose color suggests a connection with nature. The song also explicitly compares the man and woman to vegetation: the woman is a flower and the man is a fruit tree. Images of plants and frolicking animals are symbols of life, and as such they are metaphors for the procreative act of human sexual relations. The song's references to spring and the budding of plants further emphasize the budding of romantic arousal. The couple always celebrates their love in such verdant environments—in the wilderness, the vineyard, or the garden. It is in the city, where plants do not grow and the city guards are brutal, that the maiden searches for her lover but cannot find him.

The man's comparison of the maiden to a "garden locked" and "fountain sealed" establishes the relationship between chastity and femininity (4:12). The image of an enclosed garden is a metaphor for female virginity that is frequently repeated in later medieval and Renaissance literature. In the Song of Solomon, the closed garden suggests that the girl is chaste and unsullied. The man's dining in the garden implies that the two have consummated their relationship, and his invitation to the chorus to celebrate this event with feasting further indicates the completion of this rite of passage. Later, the two walk in a vineyard, and the girl remembers her earlier virginity when she was cursed to labor in the vineyard instead of enjoying it. Her memory while in the vineyard suggests the bittersweet nature of the loss of innocence.

The garden motif is reminiscent of the Garden of Eden in Genesis, where Adam and Eve enjoy God's creation prior to the emergence of human wickedness. The parallels to Eden in The Song of

Solomon suggest that the celebration of human sensuality is, itself, a good and not a wicked thing. The maiden and her lover, however, must enjoy their love within the boundaries and confines of gardens and fields. This limitation on the enjoyment of their sexual behavior is in keeping with the ongoing biblical theme that there are ethical requirements for enjoying God's promises—for Adam and Eve to remain in the garden of Eden and for the Israelites to dwell in the promised land.

PROVERBS

OVERVIEW

Proverbs is the chief volume in the biblical collection of wisdom literature, which also includes Ecclesiastes, Job, and portions of Psalms. The purpose of wisdom literature in the Bible is to teach rather than to relate a narrative. Proverbs contains thirty-one chapters, each comprised of twenty to thirty-five wise sayings that are each two poetic lines long. Most of the book is attributed to King Solomon; but, as the book itself indicates, the written teachings in their current form were probably collected no earlier than the reign of Hezekiah, King of Judah in the late eighth and early seventh centuries B.C. Other sections of the text are attributed to additional, more obscure authors. However, it is safe to say that Proverbs represents the written record of an oral tradition of wise sayings with uncertain origins.

A proverb is a short, pithy saying that usually draws a comparison between two forms of behavior in order to impart moral or religious wisdom to its receiver. Some of the wise sayings in Proverbs also take the form of enigmatic or cryptic utterances that the receiver must interpret to understand the meaning. Biblical proverbs are religious, but they focus on concrete human experiences rather than divine revelation. Nevertheless, their judgments always entail a timeless quality, like the moral of a myth or a folktale. The biblical notion of wisdom implies acquiring skill or ability in the areas of justice and moral goodness—like a craftsmen learning a craft. In fact, Proverbs frequently instructs the listener to "get" or "buy" wisdom (4:5 and 23:23). The sayings in Proverbs are often addressed to young people, who are in the process of becoming wise. It is likely that the Book of Proverbs formed part of the education for Hebrew youth after the Israelite exile and return to the promised land.

STRUCTURE

The Book of Proverbs is divided into four main sections, with three additional sections, or appendices, included at the end. The first third of Proverbs is an extended lecture spoken by the personified voice of "Wisdom." This section is the most conversational, narrative, and thematic portion of the book. Wisdom speaks in the first person and refers to the reader as "my child," instructing the reader on various topics for wise living. The voice of Wisdom assumes different forms. On the one hand, Wisdom refers to itself in feminine terms, using the pronouns "she" and "her." Wisdom describes itself as a woman standing on the city streets, crying out her warnings to the people. However, Wisdom also identifies itself with God. Pursuing Wisdom, it says, is the same thing as obeying God, and Wisdom claims to have been God's partner in creating the world.

The next three sections of Proverbs contain the proverbs of Solomon and the sayings of the wise. The list of Solomon's proverbs is made up of two lengthy sections, and the proverbs are very loosely organized by theme. The speaker usually assumes the voice and authority of a king. Many of the proverbs follow the formula of antithetical parallelism, a convention in which the proverb is stated in two poetic lines, and one line describes a type of good or wise behavior while the other describes its evil or foolish opposite. The "sayings of the wise" make up one small section and are less rhetorical, issuing more direct commands and advice to the reader.

The final three sections in Proverbs include the brief oracles of Agur and King Lemuel and a closing lesson on how to select a good wife. Agur and Lemuel's historical existence is unknown, but their cryptic sayings continue the demand for wisdom and the themes of temperance and justice that are common to the rest of Proverbs. The final passage praises all the traits of the good and "capable" wife (31:10). She is industrious, independent, strong, generous to the poor, and, most importantly, she "fears," or obeys, God (31:30). Proverbs closes by calling for her family and the community to praise her.

THEMES

Proverbs is largely concerned with the inevitability of God's justice and the importance of prudence and moderation. Solomon's proverbs maintain that wicked deeds will invariably lead to divine retribution and punishment during a person's earthly life. People who slander others will have their tongues cut off, those who are lazy will have failing crops, and undue pride will lead to an individual's downfall. One way to enjoy the favorable hand of God's justice is to practice moderation and prudence. According to the proverbs, the moderate person avoids the excesses of the foolish, including excessive drinking, eating, sleeping, gossiping, and rage. A consistent way to demonstrate wise behavior is by choosing words shrewdly and carefully. The proverbs also praise those who prepare in advance, particularly those who build their homes in preparation for later circumstances. The most important sign of wisdom and prudence, however, is obedience and reverence to one's parents.

The importance of women and femininity in Proverbs is unusual in the context of the Old Testament. In most Old Testament narratives, women play a role secondary to that of men. However, Proverbs suggests that women can use wisdom within a male-dominated society to assert their strength and independence. The final chapter gives license to the "good wife" to do everything from selling merchandise to performing home repair, and Solomon notes earlier that it is the "wise woman who builds her house" (14:1). Interestingly, the young men throughout Proverbs wander aimlessly, searching for the correct path but falling prey to seduction. Wisdom, personified as a woman, stands fast, stationed at the city gates or in the streets delivering messages as an oracle or soothsayer. The juxtaposition of feminine Wisdom with God alters the vision of God from previous biblical books, in which God appears as an angel, a group of men, or in thunder and fire. The Book of Proverbs does not suggest that God is a woman or a being with a gender. Nevertheless, the feminine voice of Wisdom claims to be an integral part of God. Wisdom notes, "The Lord created me at the / beginning of his work.... [T]hen I was beside him, like a / master worker" (8:22–30). Wisdom also affirms, "For whoever finds me finds life / and obtains favor from the Lord" (8:35). Wisdom is the source of life, a helper in creation, and a mediator between God and humankind. By assigning Wisdom a feminine quality, Proverbs suggests that femininity, in addition to masculinity, should be an important way in which we think about the order of the world.

Important Quotations Explained

1. I will make you exceedingly fruitful; and I will make nations of you, and kings shall come from you. I will establish my covenant between me and you, and your offspring after you throughout their generations, for an everlasting covenant, to be God to you and to your offspring after you. And I will give to you, and to your offspring after you, the land where you are now an alien, all the land of Canaan, for a perpetual holding; and I will be their God.

(Genesis 17:6–8)

These words, spoken by God, articulate God's covenant, or promise, with Abraham. Initially in the Genesis narrative, the interaction between God and humans seems bewildering and arbitrary. God speaks to isolated individuals and demands certain actions from them. Here, God lays out a plan for an ongoing relationship with humankind. God will be the deity of one group of people, and the rights to God's favor and blessings will pass on genetically from one man to his descendants. The rewards of this relationship will not only be a nation and a homeland for the Israelites but abundant, "fruitful" life. God's comments here serve two functions. First, the passage introduces the dominant motif of the Old Testament: the covenant unifies the biblical narrative, for everything the Israelites do from this point on represents either an affirmation or a rejection of God's promise. Second, the passage implies that the Israelites are not just any group or ethnicity, but a specific people descending from one man with a divine claim to land in the eastern Mediterranean region. Historically, the idea of the covenant was important for the Israelites in sustaining a sense of identity in the ethnic mix of the region as well as during the exile.

2. Hear, O Israel: The Lord is our God, the Lord alone. You
    shall love the Lord your God with all your heart, and with
    all your soul, and with all your might. Keep these words
    that I am commanding you today in your heart. Recite
    them to your children and talk about them when you are
    at home and when you are away, when you lie down and
    when you rise. Bind them as a sign on your hand, fix them
    as an emblem on your forehead.

    (Deuteronomy 6:4–8)

Stationed on the border of the Promised Land, Moses delivers these
instructions in his farewell address to the Israelites. In one sense, his
speech, which constitutes the Book of Deuteronomy, is redundant.
Moses reiterates many of the religious laws and commandments
already stated by God in the Book of Leviticus and the latter half
of Exodus. However, Moses is speaking to a new, younger generation of Israelites who, after wandering the desert for forty years, are
now ready to take the land sworn to them by God, a land they have
never seen. Just as the history of Israel is at a turning point, so Moses
describes the laws and the covenant in terms very different than before. Previously, the symbols of God's covenant have been external:
the rite of circumcision, the Ark of the Covenant, and various rules
for physical cleanliness. Now, Moses describes the laws as internal
to the Israelites. The religious laws are words and ideas that should
be so precious to the Israelites that they are in their "heart[s]," remaining with the people wherever they go. This passage suggests
why Judaism refers to the biblical laws as "Torah": laws that are not
just rules for behavior but models for all of life.

3. Has the Lord as great delight in burnt offerings and sacrifices,
    as in obedience to the voice of the Lord?
    Surely, to obey is better than sacrifice,
    and to heed than the fat of rams. . . .
    Because you have rejected the word of the Lord,
    he has also rejected you from being king.

    (1 Samuel 15:22–23)

The prophet Samuel pronounces this grim curse to Saul after Saul
disobeys God. Through Samuel, God has instructed King Saul to
attack the neighboring Amalekites and destroy them completely,
sparing nothing. Saul, however, has brought back the Amalekite

QUOTATIONS

flocks as booty, apparently to use as a ritual animal sacrifice to God. This seemingly benign error not only earns God's wrath but justifies the removal of Saul as king of Israel. As such, the oversight marks a turning a point in the history of Israel, permitting David's ascent to the throne. More important, the nature of Saul's error implies a new outlook on religious obedience. Obedience is not adherence to God's laws but obedience to God himself. As Samuel suggests, God honors obedience to that which is unseen—"the voice of the Lord"—more than obedience to that which is seen—physical regulations and ceremonies. Valuing the unseen over the seen is integral to the theme of radical faith in the Old Testament. Saul does not possess this faith, yet his tragic demise over such a fine distinction earns our sympathy.

4. If I sin, what do I do to you, you watcher of humanity?
   Why have you made me your target?
   Why have I become a burden to you?

(Job 7:20)

QUOTATIONS

This rhetorical question is spoken by Job after God has killed all his children and his livestock, and afflicted him with a skin disease. Job's lament is emblematic of the central question discussed by Job and his three friends. The question is a theme in the Old Testament: how can God remain good despite the fact that he allows evil and human suffering to exist? Job's friends argue that God would only afflict Job with pain if he had committed some grave act of human disobedience meriting punishment. Job, however, raises two complaints against God, the "watcher of humanity." For one, Job knows he has done nothing wrong, and he wonders what he could have done to become a "burden" to God and deserve such suffering. Second, Job asks why God is so concerned with human actions in the first place—why he watches humanity's faults and punishes them in turn. Just as Job's lament is rhetorical and open-ended, so this question and theme is not explicitly answered in the Old Testament.

5.   For everything there is a season, and a
time for every matter under heaven:
a time to be born, and a time to die;
a time to plant, and a time to pluck up what is planted;
a time to kill, and a time to heal;
a time to break down, and a time to build up;
a time to weep, and a time to laugh;
a time to mourn, and a time to dance. . . .

(Ecclesiastes 3:1–4)

These famous verses are spoken by the unnamed Teacher who investigates the meaning of life in the Book of Ecclesiastes. The poetic interlude in the Teacher's musings represents an excellent example of the parallelism that defines biblical poetry: the lyrical verse has rhythm because each line is divided into two halves, both of which mirror and oppose each other at the same time. More important, the Teacher's saying continues the pattern of doubles and opposites developed throughout the Old Testament narrative. Since God's creation in Genesis, the Old Testament depicts the world as a place of opposing forces—good versus evil, greater versus lesser, light versus dark, seen versus unseen. The Old Testament frequently reverses these opposites, showing the younger dominating over the older, the weak over the strong, and the oppressed over the powerful. This motif suggests that humans cannot confidently discern that which is better or worse without faith in God. Similarly, the Teacher explains that there is a time for every human experience, good and bad. One cannot say that dancing is obviously better than mourning, for both experiences are integral to human life. The Teacher argues that trying to find meaning in life by what people traditionally assume to be better or worse is misguided, and that the only correct way for humans to behave is to fear, or obey, God.

QUOTATIONS

KEY FACTS

FULL TITLE
The Old Testament

AUTHOR
Unknown (various)

TYPE OF WORK
Sacred writings and religious narrative

GENRE
Myth; folktale; epic; poetry; wisdom literature

LANGUAGE
Ancient Hebrew; some passages in Aramaic (an ancient Near-Eastern dialect)

TIME AND PLACE WRITTEN
First millennium B.C., Palestine and surrounding Near-Eastern regions

DATE OF FIRST PUBLICATION
Fourth century to first century B.C.

NARRATOR
The narrator of each book is anonymous, but sometimes assumes the voice of a famous biblical figure to increase the authority of a given book. For instance, in Ecclesiastes, the narrator claims to be the wise King Solomon, or the Teacher.

POINT OF VIEW
The anonymous speaker of each book typically narrates in the third person. In some books, the narrator describes events objectively (as they would appear to the observer), but the point of view is limited to the human perspective of the protagonist or of the Israelites. In others, the narrator has an omniscient, or unlimited, knowledge of both human and divine motives and actions. However, some books contain the laws and commandments spoken by God, or the lengthy speeches, poetry, and sayings of one person. These are narrated in the first person. They often contain imperatives and instructions delivered to the reader or to an unseen audience of listeners.

TONE

In the books of wisdom and law, the narrator attributes to the speaker a universal tone, as though each imperative or saying is timeless and applies to all people. In Genesis, Exodus, and the historical books, the narrator remains uncritical and withholds judgment on the characters' actions. The narrator conveys the scope of the Israelites' disobedience to God by repeating phrases or ideas that show the cyclical and ongoing nature of Israel's evil ways.

TENSE

Past

SETTING (TIME)

Approximately 2000 B.C. to 400 B.C.

SETTING (PLACE)

The Ancient Near East, particularly the eastern Mediterranean region of Palestine

PROTAGONIST

The Israelites

MAJOR CONFLICT

God promises to give the Israelite people a great land and nation, but the Israelites' persistent disobedience and worship of false gods hinders the fulfillment of God's promise, or covenant.

THEMES

The problem of evil; the possibility of redemption; the virtue of faith

MOTIFS

The covenant; doubles and opposites; geography

SYMBOLS

The fertile ground; the Ark of the Covenant

FORESHADOWING

Moses's and Joshua's exhortations to the Israelites; Israel's failure to remove the native inhabitants and their religions from the Promised Land; the division of the kingdom between Rehoboam and Jeroboam

KEY FACTS

STUDY QUESTIONS

1. *What are some of the ways God appears to humans in the Old Testament? How do these appearances change between biblical books? What do they suggest about the themes and purposes of each book?*

The various appearances of God in the Old Testament are ironic, for they frequently produce a reaction opposite to what we might expect. In Genesis, God appears in physical human form. He walks and talks with Abraham in the guise of three men, and he even wrestles with Jacob on the banks of the Jabbok River. God never identifies himself; yet by some strange faith, Jacob asks the person who has just picked a fight with him to offer him a blessing, suggesting that he knows it is God. Elijah's faith in God is similarly ironic. In the first Book of Kings, God ceases to appear to humankind because of the evil in Israel's divided kingdom. When God finally appears to Elijah, Elijah hears God's voice, not in thunder or earthquakes, but in the sound of silence—the same silence that has characterized God's absence in Israel.

These understated appearances sharply contrast God's stark appearances in the Book of Exodus. The *theophany*—or visual symbols of God—are not only supernatural but visually overwhelming. God appears as a pillar of fire, provides the Israelites with manna from heaven, and descends on Mount Sinai in a great cloud of thunder. Again, God's appearances prove ironic, but only because they fail to satisfy the Israelites, who complain and wish to return to Egypt. The failure to see God in his most convincing form proves one of the Israelites' greatest acts of disobedience. Clearly, the biblical writers tailor God's appearances to imply that true faith in God consists not in fantastic or persuasive experiences but in seeing God in one's immediate surroundings.

2. *Discuss the role of geography in the development of the biblical story. What is the relationship between physical location and religious well-being in the Old Testament?*

In one sense, Israel's proximity to the promised land mirrors its religious health. God ties the land to his covenant with the Israelites, and wherever the Israelites are located in relation to that land reflects their religious commitment to God. Enslaved in Egypt, the Israelites remain without a religion just as they are far from the promised land. The Assyrian and Babylonian exiles equally represent the outcome of Israel's persistent disobedience. Geographically, the land of Canaan falls in the middle of the ancient Near East. As such, the Old Testament describes Israel's religious story as a physical journey to and away from this geographical center. The structure of the Israelite camp in the Book of Leviticus offers an apt analogy for the relationship between geography and religious wellbeing. Israelites who are religiously "clean" may remain in the camp; but those who are ceremonially "unclean" must remain outside the camp, distancing themselves from the Ark of the Covenant at the center and, by extension, from God's blessings.

However, the Old Testament also suggests that wandering on the geographical margins is essential to religious development. Moses meets God in the form of a burning bush only after fleeing his homeland, and both Samson and David live amongst the Philistines before emerging as saviors of Israel. Wandering promotes humility, discipline, and moral probity. The Israelites learn the laws of their religion and prepare to enter the promised land by roaming the desert. Even the exile, at first emblematic of Israel's religious demise, promotes Israel's religious development. Both historically and in the Book of Esther, the exile marks the flowering of Judaism as we know it today.

3.   *Discuss the role of female characters in the Old
      Testament. To what extent do the biblical writers
      portray women in a positive or negative light?*

The Old Testament narrative depicts a male-dominated society that
was probably typical of the ancient Near East. Men are the rulers, the religious leaders, and the warriors in the nation of Israel.
Women predominantly fulfill a secondary role, as the wives or the
handmaidens of the male protagonists. The Book of Genesis defines
this role for women from the outset. God curses Eve to a life of
child-rearing and of service to her husband, Adam. Yet this curse
represents a punishment—not a blessing. The story of Eve explains
why women have a secondary role in society, but the biblical writers do not claim that this is the way life for women should or must
remain.

     Instead, the biblical writers portray women who show strength
and independence despite their marginal status. The Book of Esther
praises a young Jewish woman who, as queen of Persia, boldly
breeches rules of propriety and persuades the king to remove his
edict sanctioning the destruction of the Jews. Similarly, the Book of
Proverbs personifies Wisdom as a woman, calling out her advice to
wayward young men in the city streets. Proverbs identifies Wisdom
as a part of God's character, blurring the typical personification of
God as male. Perhaps such biblical books offer a model for the way
in which traditional hierarchies between men and women can be
reconsidered.

How to Write
Literary Analysis

The Literary Essay: A Step-by-Step Guide

When you read for pleasure, your only goal is enjoyment. You might find yourself reading to get caught up in an exciting story, to learn about an interesting time or place, or just to pass time. Maybe you're looking for inspiration, guidance, or a reflection of your own life. There are as many different, valid ways of reading a book as there are books in the world.

When you read a work of literature in an English class, however, you're being asked to read in a special way: you're being asked to perform *literary analysis*. To analyze something means to break it down into smaller parts and then examine how those parts work, both individually and together. Literary analysis involves examining all the parts of a novel, play, short story, or poem—elements such as character, setting, tone, and imagery—and thinking about how the author uses those elements to create certain effects.

A literary essay isn't a book review: you're not being asked whether or not you liked a book or whether you'd recommend it to another reader. A literary essay also isn't like the kind of book report you wrote when you were younger, where your teacher wanted you to summarize the book's action. A high school- or college-level literary essay asks, "How does this piece of literature actually work?" "How does it do what it does?" and, "Why might the author have made the choices he or she did?"

The Seven Steps
No one is born knowing how to analyze literature; it's a skill you learn and a process you can master. As you gain more practice with this kind of thinking and writing, you'll be able to craft a method that works best for you. But until then, here are seven basic steps to writing a well-constructed literary essay:

1. *Ask questions*
2. *Collect evidence*
3. *Construct a thesis*

85

4. Develop and organize arguments
5. Write the introduction
6. Write the body paragraphs
7. Write the conclusion

---

1. ASK QUESTIONS

When you're assigned a literary essay in class, your teacher will often provide you with a list of writing prompts. Lucky you! Now all you have to do is choose one. Do yourself a favor and pick a topic that interests you. You'll have a much better (not to mention easier) time if you start off with something you enjoy thinking about. If you are asked to come up with a topic by yourself, though, you might start to feel a little panicked. Maybe you have too many ideas—or none at all. Don't worry. Take a deep breath and start by asking yourself these questions:

- **What struck you?** Did a particular image, line, or scene linger in your mind for a long time? If it fascinated you, chances are you can draw on it to write a fascinating essay.

- **What confused you?** Maybe you were surprised to see a character act in a certain way, or maybe you didn't understand why the book ended the way it did. Confusing moments in a work of literature are like a loose thread in a sweater: if you pull on it, you can unravel the entire thing. Ask yourself why the author chose to write about that character or scene the way he or she did and you might tap into some important insights about the work as a whole.

- **Did you notice any patterns?** Is there a phrase that the main character uses constantly or an image that repeats throughout the book? If you can figure out how that pattern weaves through the work and what the significance of that pattern is, you've almost got your entire essay mapped out.

- **Did you notice any contradictions or ironies?** Great works of literature are complex; great literary essays recognize and explain those complexities. Maybe the title (*Happy Days*) totally disagrees with the book's subject matter (hungry orphans dying in the woods). Maybe the main character acts one way around his family and a completely different way around his friends and associates. If you can find a way to explain a work's contradictory elements, you've got the seeds of a great essay.

At this point, you don't need to know exactly what you're going to say about your topic; you just need a place to begin your exploration. You can help direct your reading and brainstorming by formulating your topic as a *question,* which you'll then try to answer in your essay. The best questions invite critical debates and discussions, not just a rehashing of the summary. Remember, you're looking for something you can *prove or argue* based on evidence you find in the text. Finally, remember to keep the scope of your question in mind: is this a topic you can adequately address within the word or page limit you've been given? Conversely, is this a topic big enough to fill the required length?

GOOD QUESTIONS

> *"Are Romeo and Juliet's parents responsible for the deaths of their children?"*
>
> *"Why do pigs keep showing up in* LORD OF THE FLIES?*"*
>
> *"Are Dr. Frankenstein and his monster alike? How?"*

BAD QUESTIONS

> *"What happens to Scout in* TO KILL A MOCKINGBIRD?*"*
>
> *"What do the other characters in* JULIUS CAESAR *think about Caesar?"*
>
> *"How does Hester Prynne in* THE SCARLET LETTER *remind me of my sister?"*

---

2. COLLECT EVIDENCE

Once you know what question you want to answer, it's time to scour the book for things that will help you answer the question. Don't worry if you don't know what you want to say yet—right now you're just collecting ideas and material and letting it all percolate. Keep track of passages, symbols, images, or scenes that deal with your topic. Eventually, you'll start making connections between these examples and your thesis will emerge.

Here's a brief summary of the various parts that compose each and every work of literature. These are the elements that you will analyze in your essay, and which you will offer as evidence to support your arguments. For more on the parts of literary works, see the Glossary of Literary Terms at the end of this section.

ELEMENTS OF STORY These are the *what*s of the work—what happens, where it happens, and to whom it happens.

- **Plot:** All of the events and actions of the work.

- **Character:** The people who act and are acted upon in a literary work. The main character of a work is known as the *protagonist.*

- **Conflict:** The central tension in the work. In most cases, the protagonist wants something, while opposing forces (antagonists) hinder the protagonist's progress.

- **Setting:** When and where the work takes place. Elements of setting include location, time period, time of day, weather, social atmosphere, and economic conditions.

- **Narrator:** The person telling the story. The narrator may straightforwardly report what happens, convey the subjective opinions and perceptions of one or more characters, or provide commentary and opinion in his or her own voice.

- **Themes:** The main idea or message of the work—usually an abstract idea about people, society, or life in general. A work may have many themes, which may be in tension with one another.

ELEMENTS OF STYLE These are the *how*s—how the characters speak, how the story is constructed, and how language is used throughout the work.

- **Structure and organization:** How the parts of the work are assembled. Some novels are narrated in a linear, chronological fashion, while others skip around in time. Some plays follow a traditional three- or five-act structure, while others are a series of loosely connected scenes. Some authors deliberately leave gaps in their works, leaving readers to puzzle out the missing information. A work's structure and organization can tell you a lot about the kind of message it wants to convey.

- **Point of view:** The perspective from which a story is told. In *first-person point of view,* the narrator involves him or herself in the story. ("I went to the store"; "We watched in horror as the bird slammed into the window.") A first-person narrator is usually the protagonist of the work, but not always. In *third-person point of view,* the narrator does not participate

LITERARY ANALYSIS

in the story. A third-person narrator may closely follow a specific character, recounting that individual character's thoughts or experiences, or it may be what we call an *omniscient* narrator. Omniscient narrators see and know all: they can witness any event in any time or place and are privy to the inner thoughts and feelings of all characters. Remember that the narrator and the author are not the same thing!

- **Diction:** Word choice. Whether a character uses dry, clinical language or flowery prose with lots of exclamation points can tell you a lot about his or her attitude and personality.

- **Syntax:** Word order and sentence construction. Syntax is a crucial part of establishing an author's narrative voice. Ernest Hemingway, for example, is known for writing in very short, straightforward sentences, while James Joyce characteristically wrote in long, incredibly complicated lines.

- **Tone:** The mood or feeling of the text. Diction and syntax often contribute to the tone of a work. A novel written in short, clipped sentences that use small, simple words might feel brusque, cold, or matter-of-fact.

- **Imagery:** Language that appeals to the senses, representing things that can be seen, smelled, heard, tasted, or touched.

- **Figurative language:** Language that is not meant to be interpreted literally. The most common types of figurative language are *metaphors* and *similes,* which compare two unlike things in order to suggest a similarity between them—for example, "All the world's a stage," or "The moon is like a ball of green cheese." (Metaphors say one thing *is* another thing; similes claim that one thing is *like* another thing.)

---

3. Construct a Thesis

When you've examined all the evidence you've collected and know how you want to answer the question, it's time to write your thesis statement. A *thesis* is a claim about a work of literature that needs to be supported by evidence and arguments. The thesis statement is the heart of the literary essay, and the bulk of your paper will be spent trying to prove this claim. A good thesis will be:

- **Arguable.** "*The Great Gatsby* describes New York society in the 1920s" isn't a thesis—it's a fact.

- **Provable through textual evidence.** "*Hamlet* is a confusing but ultimately very well-written play" is a weak thesis because it offers the writer's personal opinion about the book. Yes, it's arguable, but it's not a claim that can be proved or supported with examples taken from the play itself.

- **Surprising.** "Both George and Lenny change a great deal in *Of Mice and Men*" is a weak thesis because it's obvious. A really strong thesis will argue for a reading of the text that is not immediately apparent.

- **Specific.** "Dr. Frankenstein's monster tells us a lot about the human condition" is *almost* a really great thesis statement, but it's still too vague. What does the writer mean by "a lot"? *How* does the monster tell us so much about the human condition?

GOOD THESIS STATEMENTS

Question: In *Romeo and Juliet*, which is more powerful in shaping the lovers' story: fate or foolishness?

Thesis: "Though Shakespeare defines Romeo and Juliet as 'star-crossed lovers' and images of stars and planets appear throughout the play, a closer examination of that celestial imagery reveals that the stars are merely witnesses to the characters' foolish activities and not the causes themselves."

Question: How does the bell jar function as a symbol in Sylvia Plath's *The Bell Jar*?

Thesis: "A bell jar is a bell-shaped glass that has three basic uses: to hold a specimen for observation, to contain gases, and to maintain a vacuum. The bell jar appears in each of these capacities in *The Bell Jar*, Plath's semi-autobiographical novel, and each appearance marks a different stage in Esther's mental breakdown."

Question: Would Piggy in *The Lord of the Flies* make a good island leader if he were given the chance?

Thesis: "Though the intelligent, rational, and innovative Piggy has the mental characteristics of a good leader, he ultimately lacks the social skills necessary to be an effective one. Golding emphasizes this point by giving Piggy a foil in the charismatic Jack, whose magnetic personality allows him to capture and wield power effectively, if not always wisely."

4. Develop and Organize Arguments

The reasons and examples that support your thesis will form the middle paragraphs of your essay. Since you can't really write your thesis statement until you know how you'll structure your argument, you'll probably end up working on steps 3 and 4 at the same time.

There's no single method of argumentation that will work in every context. One essay prompt might ask you to compare and contrast two characters, while another asks you to trace an image through a given work of literature. These questions require different kinds of answers and therefore different kinds of arguments. Below, we'll discuss three common kinds of essay prompts and some strategies for constructing a solid, well-argued case.

Types of Literary Essays

- **Compare and contrast**

  Compare and contrast the characters of Huck and Jim in The Adventures of Huckleberry Finn.

  Chances are you've written this kind of essay before. In an academic literary context, you'll organize your arguments the same way you would in any other class. You can either go *subject by subject* or *point by point*. In the former, you'll discuss one character first and then the second. In the latter, you'll choose several traits (attitude toward life, social status, images and metaphors associated with the character) and devote a paragraph to each. You may want to use a mix of these two approaches—for example, you may want to spend a paragraph a piece broadly sketching Huck's and Jim's personalities before transitioning into a paragraph or two that describes a few key points of comparison. This can be a highly effective strategy if you want to make a counterintuitive argument—that, despite seeming to be totally different, the two objects being compared are actually similar in a very important way (or vice versa). Remember that your essay should reveal something fresh or unexpected about the text, so think beyond the obvious parallels and differences.

- **Trace**

  Choose an image—for example, birds, knives, or eyes—and trace that image throughout Macbeth.

  Sounds pretty easy, right? All you need to do is read the play, underline every appearance of a knife in *Macbeth,* and then list them in your essay in the order they appear, right? Well, not exactly. Your teacher doesn't want a simple catalog of examples. He or she wants to see you make *connections* between those examples—that's the difference between summarizing and analyzing. In the *Macbeth* example above, think about the different contexts in which knives appear in the play and to what effect. In *Macbeth,* there are real knives and imagined knives; knives that kill and knives that simply threaten. Categorize and classify your examples to give them some order. Finally, always keep the overall effect in mind. After you choose and analyze your examples, you should come to some greater understanding about the work, as well as your chosen image, symbol, or phrase's role in developing the major themes and stylistic strategies of that work.

- **Debate**

  Is the society depicted in 1984 good for its citizens?

  In this kind of essay, you're being asked to debate a moral, ethical, or aesthetic issue regarding the work. You might be asked to judge a character or group of characters (*Is Caesar responsible for his own demise?*) or the work itself (*Is* JANE EYRE *a feminist novel?*). For this kind of essay, there are two important points to keep in mind. First, don't simply base your arguments on your personal feelings and reactions. Every literary essay expects you to read and analyze the work, so search for evidence in the text. What do characters in *1984* have to say about the government of Oceania? What images does Orwell use that might give you a hint about his attitude toward the government? As in any debate, you also need to make sure that you define all the necessary terms before you begin to argue your case. What does it mean to be a "good" society? What makes a novel "feminist"? You should define your terms right up front, in the first paragraph after your introduction.

  Second, remember that strong literary essays make contrary and surprising arguments. Try to think outside the box. In the *1984* example above, it seems like the obvious answer would be no, the totalitarian society depicted in Orwell's novel is *not* good for its citizens. But can you think of any arguments for the opposite side? Even if your final assertion is that the novel depicts a cruel, repressive, and therefore harmful society, acknowledging and responding to the counterargument will strengthen your overall case.

LITERARY ANALYSIS

5. Write the Introduction

Your introduction sets up the entire essay. It's where you present your topic and articulate the particular issues and questions you'll be addressing. It's also where you, as the writer, introduce yourself to your readers. A persuasive literary essay immediately establishes its writer as a knowledgeable, authoritative figure.

An introduction can vary in length depending on the overall length of the essay, but in a traditional five-paragraph essay it should be no longer than one paragraph. However long it is, your introduction needs to:

- **Provide any necessary context.** Your introduction should situate the reader and let him or her know what to expect. What book are you discussing? Which characters? What topic will you be addressing?

- **Answer the "So what?" question.** Why is this topic important, and why is your particular position on the topic noteworthy? Ideally, your introduction should pique the reader's interest by suggesting how your argument is surprising or otherwise counterintuitive. Literary essays make unexpected connections and reveal less-than-obvious truths.

- **Present your thesis.** This usually happens at or very near the end of your introduction.

- **Indicate the shape of the essay to come.** Your reader should finish reading your introduction with a good sense of the scope of your essay as well as the path you'll take toward proving your thesis. You don't need to spell out every step, but you do need to suggest the organizational pattern you'll be using.

Your introduction should not:

- **Be vague.** Beware of the two killer words in literary analysis: *interesting* and *important*. Of course the work, question, or example is interesting and important—that's why you're writing about it!

- **Open with any grandiose assertions.** Many student readers think that beginning their essays with a flamboyant statement such as, "Since the dawn of time, writers have been fascinated with the topic of free will," makes them sound important and commanding. You know what? It actually sounds pretty amateurish.

- **Wildly praise the work.** Another typical mistake student writers make is extolling the work or author. Your teacher doesn't need to be told that "Shakespeare is perhaps the greatest writer in the English language." You can mention a work's reputation in passing—by referring to *The Adventures of Huckleberry Finn* as "Mark Twain's enduring classic," for example—but don't make a point of bringing it up unless that reputation is key to your argument.

- **Go off-topic.** Keep your introduction streamlined and to the point. Don't feel the need to throw in all kinds of bells and whistles in order to impress your reader—just get to the point as quickly as you can, without skimping on any of the required steps.

---

6. WRITE THE BODY PARAGRAPHS

Once you've written your introduction, you'll take the arguments you developed in step 4 and turn them into your body paragraphs. The organization of this middle section of your essay will largely be determined by the argumentative strategy you use, but no matter how you arrange your thoughts, your body paragraphs need to do the following:

- **Begin with a strong topic sentence.** Topic sentences are like signs on a highway: they tell the reader where they are and where they're going. A good topic sentence not only alerts readers to what issue will be discussed in the following paragraph but also gives them a sense of what argument will be made *about* that issue. "Rumor and gossip play an important role in *The Crucible*" isn't a strong topic sentence because it doesn't tell us very much. "The community's constant gossiping creates an environment that allows false accusations to flourish" is a much stronger topic sentence— it not only tells us *what* the paragraph will discuss (gossip) but *how* the paragraph will discuss the topic (by showing how gossip creates a set of conditions that leads to the play's climactic action).

- **Fully and completely develop a single thought.** Don't skip around in your paragraph or try to stuff in too much material. Body paragraphs are like bricks: each individual one needs to be strong and sturdy or the entire structure will collapse. Make sure you have really proven your point before moving on to the next one.

- **Use transitions effectively.** Good literary essay writers know that each paragraph must be clearly and strongly linked to the material around it. Think of each paragraph as a response to the one that precedes it. Use transition words and phrases such as *however, similarly, on the contrary, therefore,* and *furthermore* to indicate what kind of response you're making.

---

7. WRITE THE CONCLUSION

Just as you used the introduction to ground your readers in the topic before providing your thesis, you'll use the conclusion to quickly summarize the specifics learned thus far and then hint at the broader implications of your topic. A good conclusion will:

- **Do more than simply restate the thesis.** If your thesis argued that *The Catcher in the Rye* can be read as a Christian allegory, don't simply end your essay by saying, "And that is why *The Catcher in the Rye* can be read as a Christian allegory." If you've constructed your arguments well, this kind of statement will just be redundant.

- **Synthesize the arguments, not summarize them.** Similarly, don't repeat the details of your body paragraphs in your conclusion. The reader has already read your essay, and chances are it's not so long that they've forgotten all your points by now.

- **Revisit the "So what?" question.** In your introduction, you made a case for why your topic and position are important. You should close your essay with the same sort of gesture. What do your readers know now that they didn't know before? How will that knowledge help them better appreciate or understand the work overall?

- **Move from the specific to the general.** Your essay has most likely treated a very specific element of the work—a single character, a small set of images, or a particular passage. In your conclusion, try to show how this narrow discussion has wider implications for the work overall. If your essay on *To Kill a Mockingbird* focused on the character of Boo Radley, for example, you might want to include a bit in your conclusion about how he fits into the novel's larger message about childhood, innocence, or family life.

- **Stay relevant.** Your conclusion should suggest new directions of thought, but it shouldn't be treated as an opportunity to pad your essay with all the extra, interesting ideas you came up with during your brainstorming sessions but couldn't fit into the essay proper. Don't attempt to stuff in unrelated queries or too many abstract thoughts.

- **Avoid making overblown closing statements.** A conclusion should open up your highly specific, focused discussion, but it should do so without drawing a sweeping lesson about life or human nature. Making such observations may be part of the point of reading, but it's almost always a mistake in essays, where these observations tend to sound overly dramatic or simply silly.

A+ Essay Checklist

Congratulations! If you've followed all the steps we've outlined above, you should have a solid literary essay to show for all your efforts. What if you've got your sights set on an A+? To write the kind of superlative essay that will be rewarded with a perfect grade, keep the following rubric in mind. These are the qualities that teachers expect to see in a truly A+ essay. How does yours stack up?

- ✓ Demonstrates a thorough understanding of the book
- ✓ Presents an original, compelling argument
- ✓ Thoughtfully analyzes the text's formal elements
- ✓ Uses appropriate and insightful examples
- ✓ Structures ideas in a logical and progressive order
- ✓ Demonstrates a mastery of sentence construction, transitions, grammar, spelling, and word choice

Suggested Essay Topics

1. *What are some of the signs or symbols of God's covenant with humankind? How do they change over the course of the Pentateuch (the first five books of the Old Testament)?*

2. *Compare and contrast Moses and David as national and religious leaders of Israel. How are they alike in their responses to those who oppose them? How are they different?*

3. *Discuss some of the characters who experience a reversal of fortune in the Old Testament. What is common or unique about their experiences? What religious ideals does the Old Testament portray in their reversal?*

4. *What are some of the images used in biblical poetry to depict God, humans, and the conflict between good and evil? How do these metaphors continue the themes and motifs of the Old Testament?*

5. *Compare and contrast Abraham and his grandson Jacob as patriarchs, or fathers, of the Hebrew people. In what sense do their experiences foreshadow the struggles of the Israelites?*

A+ Student Essay

> Does Hebrew scripture present a consistent picture of human morality?

The early books of Hebrew scripture, Genesis and Exodus in particular, tell the story of the Israelite people's evolution from a single individual to a large nation. As part of this story, these books also show how the Israelites' perception of morality shifts over time. Though the basic tenets do not change, the increasingly complex society the Israelites live in requires a correspondingly intricate set of codes and regulations. Morality therefore evolves from a simple recognition that notions of right and wrong are necessary into an elaborate system of rules and duties, one that requires individuals to recognize that they have duties to God, to one another, and to themselves.

The problem of good and evil is present from the outset of Hebrew scripture. In the Book of Genesis, the deity Yahweh forbids Adam and Eve from approaching the Tree of Knowing Good and Evil. Yahweh wants Adam and Eve to remain ignorant of the difference between good and evil because it is that ignorance that maintains the boundary between gods and humans. If Adam and Eve eat from that tree, Yahweh says, they will "become like one of us." Adam and Eve do eat from the tree, of course, and Yahweh expels them from the paradise of his garden, though not without first making clothes for them from animal skins. This story suggests, then, that humans are different from all other animals because they recognize the importance of morality. Having a conception of right and wrong is a great achievement, but it also comes with a terrible cost, since life is made difficult precisely because we believe that there are good actions we should be undertaking. Life would be easier, perhaps even blissful, if we lacked morality, but we would be little better than animals without it.

Later in Genesis, however, the human accomplishment of morality loses some of its luster as it becomes clear that people are frequently unable to live up to their moral standards. Humans become so wicked, in fact, that Yahweh floods the Earth to rid it of his vile creations, saving only Noah and his family. After doing so, Yahweh announces that he will never do so again, since "the inclination of the human heart is evil." Yahweh realizes that it is unjust to punish humanity collectively, since he created people with a natural tendency

LITERARY ANALYSIS

to act badly. Thus Genesis reveals that while morality is a fundamental human characteristic, it is extremely difficult to live a moral life since our instincts run counter to what we believe we ought to do.

The Book of Genesis, however, is very vague about what specific actions our morality should consist of, stipulating only that Adam and Eve should not eat from the tree, that no one should commit murder, and that people should reproduce. These few guidelines may work on a very small scale but they are hardly sufficient to serve as a guide for people living in a large and complex society, so the following books of Exodus and Leviticus make up for this absence by stipulating a series of commandments—613 in total—that govern individual and community affairs. These commandments range from highly specific dictates about proper clothing, food, and herding practices, to general rules forbidding murder, theft, and adultery, and they also stipulate punishments for many of the violations they describe. In Genesis, morality has been a problem in that people have little inclination to be good on their own. Exodus presents a solution to this problem by giving people extremely detailed guidelines to follow and instilling the fear of punishment in humans as a means of encouraging them to behave morally. The growing complexity of moral law reflects the growing complexity of society, which in Exodus encompasses hundreds of thousands of people, rather than the handful of families described in Genesis.

Moreover, the Book of Exodus shows that morality consists of a wide range of duties. This view of morality is made explicit in the Ten Commandments, which depict three different kinds of obligations. The first type of duty is religious, which is embodied in the commandments to cease worshipping other gods, to stop making idols, to refrain from using Yahweh's name in vain, and to sanctify one day of the week. The commandments then move on to social obligations, requiring the Israelites to honor their parents and forbidding them to murder, commit adultery, steal, or lie. The final kind of duty that the Ten Commandments present is the duty to oneself, which is expressed in the final commandment, the prohibition on coveting. Coveting is an internal action, one that has no negative consequences on other people, but is nevertheless important to avoid as it reflects a level of dissatisfaction with oneself that Exodus presents as problematic. The development of morality across time in Hebrew scripture thus culminates in the recognition that ethical behavior in a complex society is a matter not merely of metaphysical beliefs and social actions, but of self-conception and self-awareness.

LITERARY ANALYSIS

GLOSSARY OF LITERARY TERMS

ANTAGONIST

The entity that acts to frustrate the goals of the *protagonist*. The antagonist is usually another *character* but may also be a non-human force.

ANTIHERO / ANTIHEROINE

A *protagonist* who is not admirable or who challenges notions of what should be considered admirable.

CHARACTER

A person, animal, or any other thing with a personality that appears in a *narrative*.

CLIMAX

The moment of greatest intensity in a text or the major turning point in the *plot*.

CONFLICT

The central struggle that moves the *plot* forward. The conflict can be the *protagonist*'s struggle against fate, nature, society, or another person.

FIRST-PERSON POINT OF VIEW

A literary style in which the *narrator* tells the story from his or her own *point of view* and refers to himself or herself as "I." The narrator may be an active participant in the story or just an observer.

HERO / HEROINE

The principal *character* in a literary work or *narrative*.

IMAGERY

Language that brings to mind sense-impressions, representing things that can be seen, smelled, heard, tasted, or touched.

MOTIF

A recurring idea, structure, contrast, or device that develops or informs the major *themes* of a work of literature.

NARRATIVE

A story.

NARRATOR

The person (sometimes a *character*) who tells a story; the *voice* assumed by the writer. The narrator and the author of the work of literature are not the same person.

PLOT

The arrangement of the events in a story, including the sequence in which they are told, the relative emphasis they are given, and the causal connections between events.

POINT OF VIEW

The *perspective* that a *narrative* takes toward the events it describes.

PROTAGONIST

The main *character* around whom the story revolves.

SETTING

The location of a *narrative* in time and space. Setting creates mood or atmosphere.

SUBPLOT

A secondary *plot* that is of less importance to the overall story but may serve as a point of contrast or comparison to the main plot.

SYMBOL

An object, *character,* figure, or color that is used to represent an abstract idea or concept. Unlike an *emblem,* a symbol may have different meanings in different contexts.

SYNTAX

The way the words in a piece of writing are put together to form lines, phrases, or clauses; the basic structure of a piece of writing.

THEME

A fundamental and universal idea explored in a literary work.

TONE

The author's attitude toward the subject or *characters* of a story or poem or toward the reader.

VOICE

An author's individual way of using language to reflect his or her own personality and attitudes. An author communicates voice through *tone, diction,* and *syntax.*

LITERARY ANALYSIS

A Note on Plagiarism

Plagiarism—presenting someone else's work as your own—rears its ugly head in many forms. Many students know that copying text without citing it is unacceptable. But some don't realize that even if you're not quoting directly, but instead are paraphrasing or summarizing, *it is plagiarism* unless you cite the source.

Here are the most common forms of plagiarism:

- Using an author's phrases, sentences, or paragraphs without citing the source
- Paraphrasing an author's ideas without citing the source
- Passing off another student's work as your own

How do you steer clear of plagiarism? You should *always* acknowledge all words and ideas that aren't your own by using quotation marks around verbatim text or citations like footnotes and endnotes to note another writer's ideas. For more information on how to give credit when credit is due, ask your teacher for guidance or visit www.sparknotes.com.

REVIEW & RESOURCES

QUIZ

1. Why does Cain kill his brother Abel?

   A. Because the serpent tells him to
   B. Because Abel teases Cain
   C. Because Adam loves Abel more
   D. Because God is more pleased by Abel's sacrifice than by Cain's

2. Which of the following is not a sign of God's covenant, or promise, with Abraham?

   A. The rite of circumcision
   B. God renaming Abraham and his wife Sarah
   C. God destroying the cities of Sodom and Gomorrah
   D. God providing Sarah with a son, Isaac

3. How does Jacob steal his brother Esau's inheritance rights?

   A. By killing his brother
   B. By tricking his father with the help of his mother
   C. By sleeping with his mother
   D. By exposing Esau's plan to murder his father

4. How many sons does Jacob have?

   A. Three
   B. Four
   C. Ten
   D. Twelve

5. What is Jacob's alternate name?

   A. Judah
   B. Isaac
   C. Israel
   D. Ishmael

6. From which catastrophe does Joseph save Egypt?

    A. Famine
    B. A plague
    C. Military invasion
    D. A flood

7. How does God first appear to Moses?

    A. As a group of three men
    B. As an angel
    C. As a flaming sword
    D. As a burning bush

8. What object that God gives Moses allows him to perform signs and wonders?

    A. The stone tablets
    B. A wooden staff
    C. A colorful robe
    D. A golden censer

9. How does God feed the Israelites in the desert?

    A. By miraculously providing fish from the Red Sea
    B. By a strange bread-like substance from heaven
    C. By food produced from Moses's staff
    D. By an endless supply of produce from Egypt

10. Why does Moses break the stone tablets inscribed with God's commandments at Mount Sinai?

    A. Because he trips walking down the mountain
    B. Because God commands him to
    C. Because Moses refuses to lead the people any longer
    D. Because the people are worshipping a golden idol

11. Why does God curse the Israelites to wander the desert for forty years before entering the promised land?

A. Because a group of Israelite spies incites an uprising to return to Egypt

B. Because the Israelites incorrectly perform the ritual sacrifice

C. Because the Israelites vote down Moses as their leader

D. Because the Israelites worship golden idols

12. What do Moses and Joshua forbid the Israelites to do in the promised land?

A. Intermarry with the native inhabitants

B. Conquer the cities of the region

C. Divide the land amongst the twelve tribes

D. Bathe in the Jordan River

13. Who betrays Samson to the Philistines?

A. Sarah

B. Delilah

C. Gideon

D. Deborah

14. Why does God reject Saul as king of Israel?

A. Because Saul has too many concubines

B. Because Saul kills Samuel

C. Because Saul does not completely destroy the Amalekites

D. Because Saul is too cowardly to fight the Philistines

15. Why does the prophet Nathan rebuke David?

A. David fails to build the Temple to God.

B. David curses God inadvertently.

C. David commits adultery with Bathsheba.

D. David allows one of his sons to rape his stepsister.

16. What does David bring to Jerusalem to bless the religious city?

    A. The body of Moses
    B. The Ark of the Covenant
    C. The prophet Samuel
    D. Thousands of animals to be sacrificed to God

17. How does Absalom flaunt his brief overthrow of David's throne?

    A. By destroying David's palace
    B. By killing the priests of Israel
    C. By taunting David and his army as they flee Jerusalem
    D. By sleeping with David's concubines in public

18. What event triggers the division of Israel into two kingdoms?

    A. Jeroboam desecrates the Temple in Jerusalem.
    B. Jeroboam leads a rebellion against the wicked King Rehoboam.
    C. King Solomon's sons fight over the throne.
    D. Rehoboam wants the tribe of Judah to secede from the twelve tribes.

19. Who is Elisha?

    A. Elijah
    B. Elijah's opponent
    C. Elijah's apprentice and successor
    D. Elijah's son

20. What do the deaths of King Ahab and his wife Jezebel have in common?

    A. Elijah stabs them in their sleep.
    B. Dogs eat the blood of their dead bodies.
    C. The Philistines gouge out their eyes.
    D. They die cursing God.

21. Which Jewish festival results from the events in Esther?

 A. Passover
 B. Hanukkah
 C. Purim
 D. Rosh Hashanah

22. Which of the following is not one of Israel's judges?

 A. Deborah
 B. Gideon
 C. Ahab
 D. Jephthah

23. What does King Solomon do in Israel?

 A. He introduces animal sacrifices.
 B. He bans the cult of Baal worship in Israel.
 C. He builds a grand temple in Jerusalem.
 D. He forms a legendary round table of leaders and priests.

24. What is one of the main criteria in Leviticus for living in the Israelite camp?

 A. To be ceremonially clean
 B. To remain sexually abstinent
 C. To be a religious priest
 D. Not to shave

25. Why does God reprimand Job?

 A. Because Job listens to his wife and curses God
 B. Because Job does not delight in his suffering
 C. Because Job uses human knowledge to question God's ways
 D. Because Job heeds the advice of his friends

ANSWER KEY

1: D; 2: C; 3: B; 4: D; 5: C; 6: A; 7: D; 8: B; 9: B; 10: D; 11: A; 12: A;
13: B; 14: C; 15: C; 16: B; 17: D; 18: B; 19: C; 20: B; 21: C; 22: C;
23: C; 24: A; 25: C

SUGGESTIONS FOR FURTHER READING

ALTER, ROBERT and FRANK KERMODE, eds. *The Literary Guide to the Bible.* Cambridge, MA: Harvard University Press, 1987.

AUERBACH, ERICH. "Odysseus' Scar." *Mimesis: The Representation of Reality in Western Literature.* Trans. Willard R. Trask. Princeton, NJ: Princeton University Press, 1953.

BARTON, JOHN and JOHN MUDDIMAN, eds. *The Oxford Bible Commentary.* New York: Oxford University Press, 2001.

FREEDMAN, DAVID NOEL, ed. *Eerdmans Dictionary of the Bible.* Grand Rapids, MI: W. B. Eerdmans Publishing Company, 2000.

JAGERSMA, HENK. *A History of Israel in the Old Testament Period.* Trans. John Bowden. Philadelphia: Fortress Press, 1983.

MILES, JACK. *God: A Biography.* New York: Vintage Books, 1995.

NOTH, MARTIN. *The History of Israel.* 2nd ed. Trans. P. R. Ackroyd. New York: Harper and Row, 1960.